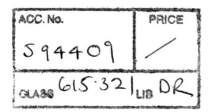
MacFarlane's Health Remedies
by M K MacFarlane

First published in Great Britain MCMXCV by Carnell plc,
28 Eccleston Square, London SW1V 1PA.

Typeset by SJ Design and Publishing, Bromley, Kent.
Printed by Repro City Limited, London.

ISBN 1-85779-577-6

TABLE OF CONTENTS

TO THE READER

This book and the views, opinions and advice expressed in it should not be used as a substitute or relied upon for medical diagnosis. You are advised always to consult your doctor or other qualified medical practitioner for specific information and advice upon health matters. Whilst every effort has been made to ensure accuracy the publisher cannot accept responsibility or liability for the information set out in this book nor for any of the opinions or advice expressed therein.

INTRODUCTION

Since the beginning of time mankind has sought to cure disease by a variety of means. Many of the methods that have survived have done so because they have proven themselves to be effective. Folk medicine and magic have gone hand-in-hand in the treatment of disease. Particular ethnic or geographic groups of people have relied on the things readily available to treat illness. At one extreme are the traditional medicines of India and China, which both have a large body of theory based on centuries of observation and associations with complex cosmological systems – and at the other extreme are the simple health practices handed down within individual families.

Much folk medicine deals with emotional needs of the patient that may be related to their bodily ailments. For example, the American Indian medicine man was often observed to involve the patient's family and tribe in such a way that personal conflicts were resolved while the patient recovered their physical health. The tribal members often offered gifts to the patient and sometimes the curative ritual involved a family member with whom the patient had quarrelled.

Although many practices of folk medicine are based at least in part on religion, superstition or social customs, many of them have also been found empirically to work reliably. The complex cultural-empirical origins of some folk practices often obscure their therapeutic value for observers who have approached the practices from the viewpoint of another culture or of science alone. For example, a plant revered as a sacred being – the cocoa tree of South America – produces leaves that were used for medical and religious purposes by the ancient Incas. The value of cocoa leaves was not generally recognised by outsiders until an 'active principle', the analgesic cocaine, was isolated in the 19th century. The use of a spider web draped over a wound to stop bleeding or the eating of certain herbs to cure the symptoms of scurvy (also known today as vitamin C deficiency) are examples of practices known to have been in use ages before scientific studies of clotting mechanisms or vitamin deficiencies 'explained' their actions.

The modern practitioner of medicine often finds that respect for, and a certain amount of acceptance of local folk practices, are required in the medical arts – and conflicts between local customs and scientific practices may be responsible for the failure of an individual of a particular background to comply with the doctor's instructions.

Ancient remedies, such as the use of herbs, were often unfamiliar to outsiders who often did not have those particular herbs growing in their home localities. For example, the herb foxglove (Digitalis purpurea) was used by the Indians as a remedy for dropsy (fluid in the legs, often due to heart failure) and was used at least 400 years before William Withering in England discovered that it contributed the active ingredient in a local folk healer's cure for that condition. Now known as digitalis, the foxglove extract is a powerful cardiac drug.

Over 200 indigenous drugs used by the American Indian have been given official recognition by inclusion in the *Pharmacopoeia of the United States* and the *British National Formulary* at one time or another. Examples are witchhazel, podophyllum, sarsaparilla, and tobacco (for toothaches). Some of the best-known were discovered by residents of South America, such as curare, ipecac and quinine.

Many folk medicines have been based on foods. Substances used for maintaining health and treating disease have included almost every known food, but it is interesting to note that a great variety of folk medicines have all included honey, cider vinegar, lemon juice, castor and corn oil.

Several folk theories were based on a balance of body systems, such as a hot-cold system traditional in Latin America, originating from traditional Hippocratic theories concerning the need to balance the four humours of the body: blood, phlegm, black and yellow bile. Hot medicines were prescribed for cold diseases and cold medicines for hot diseases.

Chinese traditional medicine is probably the oldest body of medical knowledge. The concepts of health and disease in Chinese medicine are based on equilibrium and represent the need for balance between opposing forces. The yin and yang – are principles believed to permeate all nature. Health is seen as harmony between the two forces, illness as an imbalance or disequilibrium.

Unlike modern medicine, which often seeks an absolute change (known as a cure) these traditional medicines seek to restore a healthy balance between opposing forces.

Cartesian dualism gradually tilted the efforts of doctors towards bodily processes only, since the mind remained incomprehensible. Structure, function and internal disease processes came to the centre of medical attention, while environmental and behavioural factors associated with health faded into the background. An engineering approach to human health and disease slowly evolved, with the body being treated as a group of mechanical systems that would break down and then have to be repaired.

Spurred on by the successes in the physical sciences from Galileo to Newton, doctors sought to establish their own laws governing the phenomena of health and sickness. The physical and chemical discoveries were brought together and integrated into new theoretical frameworks capable of guiding the curing of disease as if the human body were a piece of equipment, separated from the mind.

Nosology, the systematic classification of disease, became an important medical task. It was assumed that diseases had an independent reality and could be arranged and codified into fixed categories just like plants and animals. This meant that doctors had to abstract from each patient essential symptoms and features to construct a model of the disease – ignoring the patient's ethnic or cultural background and the impact their thoughts had on their disease process.

Since the time of Hippocrates, environmental factors had been recognised as influencing infectious disease, with those causative factors known as 'wormy seeds' or 'ferments'. One of the fundamental advances in 19th-century medicine was the discovery and acceptance of the germ theory of disease.

Treatment with radiation for cancers and with chemical compounds that selectively destroyed infective micro-organisms began in the early 1900s, and the introduction of penicillin opened new areas of inquiry leading to the discovery of numerous substances with antibiotic activity.

Now the clinical laboratory, applying chemistry, the microscope and high-tech diagnostic techniques to the patient's blood or tissue samples have elevated laboratory medicine from merely a handmaiden to a fully-fledged partner of doctors.

Unfortunately, while this complex diagnostic and treatment method is necessary for some ailments, it can become over-kill for things that only need a little balancing or adjusting. Often the overworked practitioner, who is routinely dealing with life- threatening illnesses, may find the minor complaints of patients easily dismissible – or treatable with readily written prescriptions – often with undesirable side-effects.

Many would wish to find something in Nature that has been proven to be effective – that doesn't require a prescription – but perhaps might require a little effort on the part of the patient. Often that something is outside the experience of the doctor who has become accustomed to high-tech answers to medical problems. Often the patient, once 'cured' by high-tech medicine, might wish for something else to continue the recovery or to assure that the illness will not return.

Modern-day medicine is fantastic and none of us would wish to return to the days of leeches and blood-letting. However, it would be wonderful to combine the wonders of modern diagnosis and treatment with the humaneness of self-assistance. In our pursuit of science we have wandered away from doing things to help ourselves and relied on science and the doctor to cure us.

Many of the suggestions contained in this book have been used by thousands of people to cure themselves and just like a wonder drug, they have found them to be simple, easily understood and virtually risk-free.

Many of us know that we can aid in our recovery with positive thoughts and the aid of Nature and time. It is to this group that this book is addressed – those who wish to try to add something to their modern-day treatment themselves.

To those who might want to take something natural or to do something positive to aid in their recovery while still following the direction of their doctor, and who are willing to work with Nature to aid themselves in their recovery, we direct these beneficial hints. Much can be added to the treatment by the patient without interference with the prescribed treatment of the doctor and many will find their health improved by so doing.

The doctor is not responsible for your health or your recovery. You are.

If you feel some of the remedies in this book will help you – or you would like to try them and see if they make a difference – introduce them slowly. Observe your body – ask yourself if the treatment makes you feel better, feel worse, or doesn't make any change at all. Pay attention to your body and the results you are getting.

Everyone is different. Let your body tell you whether or not a particular hint or remedy is right for you. Give these natural additions to your treatment a little time, Nature works slowly, whether producing a carrot or correcting a deficiency.

If the remedy you are trying doesn't seem to help you and make a difference in your illness, fine. Discontinue it and go on to something else.

It is a good idea to remember the old adage: Everything in moderation.

* * * *

Following are some methods for applying natural remedies which you may find helpful when using the hints in this book.

A **POULTICE** can be made of vegetables, fruits or herbs. These ingredients are usually chopped, crushed or mashed, softened with hot water, wrapped in a clean cloth and then applied externally to the affected area.

An **INFUSION** or **TEA** can be made by placing the ingredient in a cup and pouring boiling water over it. The ingredient itself should not be boiled as certain vitamins and active principles are unstable when exposed to such extreme heat. Let it steep for several minutes, the longer the stronger, and then strain before drinking. If the herb or ingredient is bitter, it can be sweetened with a little raw honey which is preferable to sugar. Sugar is said to decrease the medicinal value of most herbs.

A **BATH** or **SOAK** is prepared by placing a handful of the ingredient in a cloth and securing the ends. Toss the cloth into the bath and let the water run over it before enjoying the soak.

An **OINTMENT**, **CREAM** or **SALVE** is prepared by adding the ingredient to a solid fat, such as lard or cocoa butter, as a vehicle to keep the ingredient in contact with the skin.

An **UNGUENT** is an ointment made with a liquid fat, such as olive oil.

A **DRAWING SALVE** (for boils and splinters) can be made with chaparral, comfrey, chickweed or goldenseal.

A **GENERAL HEALING SALVE** (for cuts and scrapes, nappy rash, cracked lips and nipples, chapped and dry skin, insect bites and itching) can be made with comfrey, chickweed.

A **MOISTURISING AND BURN OINTMENT** (for burns, sunburn, chapped hands and face, psoriasis, hives, itching, and acne) can be made with aloe vera with comfrey, wheatgerm oil, almond oil and olive oil.

A **PAIN-RELIEVING SALVE** (for minor aches and pains of muscles and joints, backache, arthritis, neuralgia, bruises, and sprains) can be made from eucalyptus oil, camphor oil, wintergreen oil and peppermint.

Dedication:

To the memory of
May Young Johnstone

ACNE

It is the evening you have been waiting for but what is that in the middle of your forehead – and on your chin – AND your right cheek? Oh, NO! Huge, ugly pimples!

Skin is the largest organ of the body and just when teenagers become aware of the opposite sex, increased hormonal activity causes the glands which lubricate the skin to increase in activity. The result: whiteheads, blackheads and reddened pimples begin to sprout on the shoulders, back, neck and face.

Acne is a complex process created by an interaction between hormones, the oil and wax of the glands of the skin, and bacteria.

Blackheads form when the sebum combines with skin pigments and plugs the openings of the pores. If scales below the surface of the skin become filled with sebum, whiteheads are the result. When the whiteheads build up, spread under the skin and rupture, large pimples can be the result.

Heredity plays a role in the activity of these glands.

Fortunately, often by the mid-twenties, acne will no longer be a problem. Stress, sun exposure and seasonal changes can often bring on an outbreak.

- Keep your face clean, but not scrubbed. Wash your face thoroughly every night before going to bed (oil-based make-up should be avoided) so that make-up and the debris of the day on the skin is removed.
- Wash your face again in the morning because metabolic activity during the night has brought impurities to the surface which should be removed before anything is done to the skin (applying make-up, or for men, shaving).
- Keep your hair clean and off your face.
- Clean hands are a must. Touching the face is one of the biggest contributors of bacteria which then interact with the facial oils.
- Do not pick or remove blackheads as this can cause enlarged pores.
- Pay attention to what you eat. Despite the claims of dermatologists that acne has nothing to do with diet, lots of people have observed that their acne is aggravated by certain foods. Chocolate, nuts, coffee, fried foods and cola drinks are some things that are commonly implicated.
- Avoid animal fats. A few naturopathic physicians believe that a diet low in animal fats is the key to curing acne. Other researchers have concluded that high-fat diets have an adverse effect on the utilisation of zinc in the diet.
- Increase your intake of raw vegetables.

- Use an over-the-counter preparation with benzoyl peroxide.
- You might want to try the juice of 2 garlic cloves mixed with an equal amount of vinegar on the blemish at bedtime.
- Or, apply the juice of one cucumber to the entire face and leave on for 15 minutes, rinse off.
- Treat blackheads with lemon juice at bedtime, rinse off in the morning.

You need to continue these regimes for several weeks to see any results, so be patient.

AGE SPOTS

You don't mind telling a little white lie about your true age but those little brown spots can give your age away. Everyone hates them, because they tell the world you are old!

These flat brown spots (also called liver spots) are a result of the accumulation of waste build-up known as lipofuscin, a by-product of free radical damage.

- Try a concealer that matches your skin tone.
- Increase your intake of vitamin C to 500 mg daily as a free radical scavenger to stop the production of additional spots.
- Increase the amount of raw fruits and vegetables in your diet.
- Avoid exposure to the sun, always use a sunscreen with a SPF of 15, even on overcast days.
- Avoid caffeine and the ingestion of rancid oils.
- Use an over-the-counter bleaching cream.
- You might want to try a mixture of 1 teaspoonful of onion juice mixed with 2 teaspoonfuls of vinegar applied to the spot twice daily.
- Or puncture 1 capsule of vitamin E and rub onto the spot at bedtime.

AGEING SUCCESSFULLY

You tell great jokes, you can still dance the night away, your garden looks great, and you brag that you can still remember everything a lot of your friends have forgotten. Nobody wants to be considered 'old', and chronological age is unimportant, as long as you remain active, vigorous and self-sufficient.

Successful ageing involves many factors within your control – your attitudes, activities and relationships. No matter what stage of the ageing process you're in right now, you can make lifestyle changes that will help.

- Anticipate and accommodate. Plan for retirement: successful ageing means making plans for what you will do after you retire. How will you spend your days?

- Structure your days. It will give your life meaning.
- Set priorities to avoid stress.
- Have some daily goals and some life goals. It gives you a sense of excitement about the future and a feeling of success when you attain a predetermined goal.
- Have diverse interests. Balance solitary activities with group activities. Think about adapting, rather than giving up favourite pastimes if they are too strenuous.
- Expand your horizons. Learning something new is always exciting.
- Accept your limitations. So you can't dance the limbo anymore, but you probably can still waltz.
- Stay in touch with distant friends. They can remember a lot of the same experiences you do.
- Share memories with grandchildren. They will enjoy your stories of the past if you tell them well.
- You do not need to be rich to be happy. Try to budget for activities and a lifestyle that you value.
- Draw upon the kinship of others. Get support and encouragement from your family and friends.
- Make new friends, attend activities for people with similar interests. Take classes at your local college.
- Maintain your faith. Participating in religious services brings you into contact with people of other ages and walks of life. Faith can provide a sense of continuity and offer peace of mind.
- Maintain a positive, optimistic outlook. No matter how bad things are, there is usually a swing of the pendulum.
- Don't dwell on the negative. Nobody wants to be around a grumpy old person.
- Be engaged in the world around you. Volunteer where you can.
- Be flexible. Change will always continue. An ability to roll with the punches and a sense of humour are tools that can help you cope.
- Practice good health habits. Look for ways to incorporate regular exercise into your daily routine. Eat a balanced diet: many nutrients can slow the ageing process. Get adequate rest.
- Avoid alcohol, smoking. They only make you feel bad and slow down your thinking.

AIDS

AIDS has been called the 'black plague' of this era. Acquired immune deficiency syndrome (AIDS) is caused by a virus that destroys the immune system.

At the present time, there is no cure, so it is best to protect yourself against infection.

- Know your sexual partner. If you suspect your partner has had previous multiple partners, ask. Remember, you will be having sex with your sexual partner's previous partners for the past 10 years when it comes to this virus.
- Do not use intravenous drugs.
- Avoid sexual activities that could tear the vagina or rectum.
- Insist on the use of a condom. When used correctly, condoms will protect both partners.
- Choose condoms made of latex.
- Avoid condoms described as 'ultrathin'.
- Do not store condoms in hot or humid conditions as they can deteriorate.
- Do not use oil-based lubricants such as petroleum jelly or vegetable oil, as they may cause condoms to break.
- The condom should be held against the base of the penis after ejaculation until complete withdrawal.

ALLERGY, SEASONAL

Your nose itches, your eyes are runny, you sneeze and complain about your allergies. You feel like you have a cold that lasts all year long.

There are as many things to be allergic to as there are individuals on this planet, so allergies need to be handled on a one-to-one basis. However, many allergies are caused by things in our daily environment.

The spring type of allergic reaction is often due to tree pollens (eg oak, elm, maple); summer type, to grass pollens (eg timothy, sweet vernal, orchard) and to weed pollens (eg sheep's sorrel, English plantain); the autumn type, to weed pollens (eg ragweed).

- Air-condition your house. If your windows are open the same things that bother you outside are now inside.
- Install an air cleaner; it will take the pollen particles out of the air.
- Try an over-the-counter antihistamine without factors that can make you

sleepy (ask advice from your pharmacist).
- Isolate pets. If they have the run of the house, at least keep pets out of the bedroom.
- A diet of fresh fruits and vegetables, grains and yoghurt will aid in reducing the irritability and insomnia.
- Avoid sugar, tobacco, coffee and chocolate as sometimes these products contribute an additional silent allergic factor.
- Identify your personal allergy season, when your symptoms are at their worst.
- Pinpoint the offender and then take measures to reduce your exposure.
- Remove carpeting, as it is the perfect home for dust mites and moulds.
- Use synthetic pillows because they can be washed in hot water.
- Wash other bedding frequently, including the mattress pad.
- Watercress is said to aid in resisting allergic attacks, so add some to salads and sandwiches.
- Bananas are also said to contain chemicals which aid in building resistance to allergens: try eating one or two a day.

ALZHEIMER'S DISEASE

Does grandma put on her hat while still in her dressing-gown and head out of the door to go to the shops? Does she sometimes seem to not remember who you are?

If someone you care about appears to be showing signs of Alzheimer's disease, they should get a medical evaluation. Not everything that appears to be this disease is. Alzheimer's disease is an irreversible decrease in memory, usually beginning in the fifth or sixth decade. It is a degenerative disease of the brain which is characterised by mental deterioration that interferes with the person's ability to function. Memory loss, severe mood swings, personality changes, disoriented perceptions of space and time and the inability to concentrate and communicate follow. Ultimately the individual's health will progressively deteriorate until they are totally incapacitated.
- Orient the person to time and place daily.
- Control activities so that the individual does not wander away.
- Provide a nutritious diet. Alzheimer's sufferers often forget to eat.

Recent studies indicate that the more mentally active you are throughout life, the less likely you are to be diagnosed with Alzheimer's. The synapses, the connections that allow one brain cell to communicate with another, are always changing as a result of input. Some synapses grow stronger with new learning, some weaker with disuse. Unused connections disappear while new ones occur with the formation of new memories. The more experiences a person has, the more connections are formed between brain cells.

It is recommended that everyone:

- Read something every day.
- Write something every day.
- Engage in a challenging hobby.
- Play some word games.
- Join clubs with people who have common interests.
- Choose physical activities that are mentally challenging.
- Stay involved with others, meet new people, travel, find ways to be helpful to others.

AMNIOCENTESIS

You have waited so long for this baby and now you are worried that it might not be as healthy as you would like.

Amniocentesis can detect a number of birth defects and is justified when:

- The pregnant woman is 35 years old or more.
- Someone in the parents' immediate family has a genetic disorder.
- There is a family history of haemophilia or spina bifida.
- An earlier pregnancy produced a baby with chromosome abnormalities.

The test itself presents some risk – there is about 1 chance in 400 that it may produce a miscarriage.

ANAEMIA

You are pale, listless and feeling weak. Almost everything is too much trouble, even getting out of bed in the morning. It could be anaemia.

Iron deficiency anaemia is the most common type. Because it is the red blood cell that carries oxygen throughout the body, the effects are caused by a lack of oxygen in the tissues and the resultant attempts by the heart and lungs to compensate for this lack.

Adolescent girls with marginal iron stores may become iron-deficient from menstruation.

- Avoid beer, ice-cream and soft drinks as they contain additives that interfere with iron absorption.

- Tannins in tea, polyphenols in coffee and cadmium from cigarettes also all interfere with iron absorption and should be avoided.
- Eat more food sources of iron such as green, leafy vegetables, liver, poultry, fish, wheat germ, fruit and iron-fortified cereal. Other foods boost iron absorption such as citrus fruit, tomatoes and strawberries.
- For snacks, choose raisins or a couple of dried apricots.

ANGER

You yell, you throw things, you break the good china. Sometimes you nag. Sometimes you cry uncontrollably, you are just SO angry.
- Count to 10 and take some deep breaths.
- Take a walk, particularly if you feel you want to hit someone.
- Try to discuss it calmly, once you have calmed down.
- Listen to music, do the multiplication tables in your head, anything that will distract you, when you cannot do anything about the thing that angers you. Cursing and yelling at other drivers only keeps you agitated.

ANGINA

It isn't a heart attack nor heartburn but – a pain grips your chest when you exert yourself and then shortly after resting it is gone again.

You have been warned that you need to change your lifestyle or it will be a heart attack. So take heart – and make some lifelong lifestyle changes.
- Kick the smoking habit.
- Control the level of fat in your diet, cutting back to less than 30 per cent of your calories from fat.
- Avoid large, heavy meals.
- Rest after eating.
- Avoid exposure to cold, windy weather.
- Exercise gently and then gently increase your exercise.
- Learn to relax.
- Take an aspirin a day as it appears to prevent the activation of the blood-clotting mechanism.
- Elevate your head three or four inches at night to sleep. Sleeping in this position keeps more blood down in the legs.
- If you do get an angina attack at night, sit on the edge of the bed and put your feet on the floor.

ANXIETY

Your car won't start and you are late for work. You begin to pace back and forth and wring your hands. You feel your anxiety level rising and you don't know what you are going to do. Don't panic, your reaction is normal.

Anxiety can be a normal, often beneficial, reaction to many events. Anxiety increases your alertness and can spur you to action. Mild apprehension can give a performer or athlete that extra boost to succeed.

But if dread, apprehension or tension preoccupy your days and disturb your sleep, you are too anxious. The issues and circumstances that can cause concern are:

- ☐ **Health** – You worry about the chances of you or a loved one becoming ill.
- ☐ **Finances** – A fixed income or loss of earning power may produce worry.
- ☐ **Safety** – A feeling of vulnerability, watching TV reports about crime, diminished hearing and sight can add to this feeling.
- ☐ **Loss** – The death of a spouse or friend, or the loss of a family home can make you feel apprehensive.
- ☐ **Role change** – Retirement or the empty nest syndrome may cause you to question your worth and purpose.
- ☐ **Isolation** – Loneliness and isolation can aggravate anxiety.
- Anxiety can express itself in various ways. You may:
    - ☐ Have trouble falling asleep and staying asleep.
    - ☐ Dwell on a particular situation and find it difficult to think about something else.
    - ☐ Feel tense, restless, jittery, dizzy and sweaty.
    - ☐ Have trouble concentrating.
    - ☐ Overeat or lose your appetite.
    - ☐ Be overly vigilant and startle easily. Have a feeling of impending disaster.
    - ☐ Be depressed (anxiety can mask depression).
- When anxiety becomes an annoying part of your daily life, it is time to reassert your control. Your emotions and how you cope with life's stresses play a role in your physical health.
- Anxiety can cause or worsen an illness. It can play a role in the following:
    - ☐ Heart conditions.
    - ☐ Headaches.

- ☐   Irritable bowel syndrome.
- ☐   Dermatitis.
- ☐   Tics.
- ☐   Tremors.
- ☐   Speech impediments.
- Deep breathing can be an immediate aid when faced with a stressful situation.
- Avoid smoking, alcohol and drugs.
- Talk about your problem. Tell someone about your concern. Sharing your burden may lighten your load.
- Do something you enjoy. A pleasant activity will help distract your mind and relax you.
- Get enough rest. A good night's sleep is restorative and leaves you better able to cope.
- Exercise regularly. Physical exercise can relax you and help you to go to sleep promptly.
- Eat properly. Good nutrition may be a buffer against anxiety.
- Plan your time. A day with too much or too little to do may aggravate anxiety.
- Accept reality, it can be liberating.
- Get involved. Help yourself by helping others.
- Dress in cheery colours. They can help lift your mood.
- Fruit juice is known to be calming. Sip the one you prefer throughout the day.
- Pour 2 cupfuls of Epsom salts into a warm bath and just try relaxing for half an hour without interruptions.
- Sage tea is known to have a calming effect. Try drinking several cups a day.
- If none of these actions help you feel calmer, or if your anxiety is growing more intense, it is time to discuss it with a professional.

ARTHRITIS

Who hasn't awakened in the morning and felt as if it was just too difficult to get out of bed? Sometimes we complain about our 'arthritis' without really knowing that we have it. We just feel pain and stiffness in our joints and muscles.

Individuals should avoid deciding that because they have some aches or pains, or stiffness when they get up in the morning, that they have arthritis. Arthritis needs a proper diagnosis.

Arthritis is a chronic syndrome with symmetric inflammation of the joints which results in progressive destruction of these structures. Arthritis appears to be more than one disease. It is estimated that there are approximately 100 different types of the disease which is described loosely as 'arthritis'.

The two most common types are osteoarthritis and rheumatoid arthritis.

Osteoarthritis is related to the wear and tear of ageing and the deterioration of the cartilage at the ends of the bones. Usually this will apply to one area of the body, such as the knee or neck.

Rheumatoid arthritis is an inflammatory process that attacks the synovial membranes surrounding the lubricating fluid in the joint. The entire body is usually affected and it will create stiffness, swelling, fatigue, weight loss, fever and often crippling pain.

- Lose weight. The more overweight you are, the more stress and pressure placed on joints.
- Stretch gently and daily for greater mobility. Moving may hurt but not moving is even worse for your joints.
- Work on stress relief, as stress tightens muscles, making pain worse.
- Use a muscle ointment at bedtime so you will be less stiff when you get up in the morning.
- Try exercising in the pool. You are more flexible there and the buoyancy of the water will make movement easier.
- Use ice on a joint that has been overworked.
- Use heat when the joint is hot, swollen or tender.
- Many arthritics respond to an ingredient in fish oil, omega-3 fatty acids.
- Increase vitamin C to 500 mg a day.
- Avoid the nightshade vegetables (green peppers, aubergines, tomatoes, white potatoes) as they contain sotanine which interferes with muscle enzymes.
- Avoid supplements containing iron as it is suspected to be involved in joint pain.
- Try a low-fat diet, rich in fruits and vegetables. Often people will find that they have improvement in as little as two weeks on such a diet.
- The person with arthritis should avoid alcohol, caffeine, tobacco and excess sugar.

Many arthritis sufferers have found some simple home remedies to be beneficial – you might try a few, such as:

- Eat cherries and drink cherry juice throughout the day for four days, then stop for four days and begin again. It is thought that the cherries reduce uric acid levels. It has been reported that this will aid the arthritic bumps on the knuckles to disappear.
- Eat a portion of fresh string beans every day. String beans aid in decreasing the acid levels of the body.
- Make a tea of parsley and drink several cupfuls throughout the day.
- Rub a freshly cut clove of garlic on the painful joint and add fresh garlic to your meals. It is thought that the garlic works as an anti-inflammatory.
- Apple cider vinegar has been used for centuries as a relief for arthritis. Drink a glass of water containing several teaspoonfuls of apple cider vinegar.

Don't expect to see any results for at least one month. Give these remedies time to work.

ASTHMA

You wheeze and can't breathe – there is never a good time to have an asthma attack. Millions suffer the wheezing, chest tightness and breathing difficulties that typify asthma. A great variety of triggers can set off an asthma attack.

Folk medicine is rich in legends of remedies that have been used around the world. So go ahead and try a few of them if you must, such as one everyone seems to have heard of:

- Get a chihuahua (a very short-haired Mexican dog.) The theory seems to be that the disease will leave your body and jump to the poor dog. In reality, this has been effective, particularly with children. Psychologists think that children focus on the animal instead of their feelings of being unable to breathe and sometimes improve.

Here are some further things that have proven to be effective.

- Avoidance of the triggering stimuli.
- Examine your environment and remove dust, mould, cat and dog dander.
- Avoid smokers and smoke-filled rooms.
- Those whose asthma is triggered by cold air should avoid breathing through their mouth and cover their mouth with a scarf in winter as the nasal passages will warm the outside air.
- There is striking evidence that techniques of progressive relaxation can be used to avert an asthma attack.
- Exercise with brief periods of rest.

- Avoid foods that contain sulphites, a preservative, found in such things as shellfish and wine.
- Use a humidifier to moisturise the air in your home.
- Eucalyptus or horehound brewed as a tea act as natural bronchodilators, or airway relaxers.
- Avoid dairy products, as they produce mucus.
- Prepare equal amounts of chicory, celery and carrot juice in a juicer or blender. Drink one glassful of juice daily.
- Begin with 1 clove of garlic daily (or the equivalent in odourless garlic capsules) and slowly increase until the intake is 6 to 10 cloves daily.
- Mix 1 teaspoonful of grated horseradish with 1 teaspoonful of honey and swallow it down, followed by a large glass of room temperature water.
- At the first sign of an attack, saturate several strips of cloth with white vinegar and wrap them around both wrists loosely. This is said to stop a full blown attack of asthma from developing.

ATHLETE'S FOOT

Those hot, tired and sweaty feet! The average pair of those hard-working feet that carry us around so faithfully give off about $^1/_2$ pint of perspiration daily.

Athlete's foot is caused by a fungus that grows in such a warm and damp environment. Our poor feet probably weren't meant to be encased in those shoes for hours each day. Probably we should be walking barefoot on a sandy beach somewhere, since the fungus is killed by sunlight – but since we probably won't be, we need to keep our feet clean and dry to avoid the itchy fungus from making our feet miserable.

Athlete's foot fungus feeds from the dead skin cells and calluses of the feet, especially the skin between the toes.

- Take a daily multiple vitamin B capsule. An individual who is lacking in these vitamins is more likely to get athlete's foot.
- Wear shower shoes or foot covering in public places such as gyms or swimming pools.
- Keep the feet clean and dry particularly between the toes. Do not share towels.
- Change socks daily and wear only absorbent cotton ones. Wash all socks with white vinegar.
- Air shoes after wearing and dust feet with garlic powder before putting on your socks.

- At home expose the feet to air, wear sandals or some type of foot covering that provides ventilation as often as possible.
- Squeeze the juice from 1 large onion and massage into the infected areas of the feet. Allow to dry and then rinse. Repeat morning and evening.

BACK PAIN

So many people say, "Oh, my aching back!", that it is almost a universal complaint. It is estimated that 8 out of 10 people will have back pain at some time in their lives.

Our lifestyles are a large contributor to that aching back. Back pain which is not due to disc problems or osteoarthritis is generally due to poor posture and walking habits, high-heeled shoes, improper lifting of heavy objects, or sleeping on a mattress that does not give proper support.

If your back is giving you problems, no more than three days bedrest is beneficial. After that, the muscles that support the spine begin to be affected by disuse and this will only prolong the problem. Once you are able to move, a series of back exercises, done gently, will begin to bring the back into better condition.

- Get proper support and alignment from your shoes. If you are wearing high heels, alternate with low heels and see if it doesn't make a difference.
- If you sit at your job, get up every hour, walk around and stretch.
- If you lift on your job, learn to do it with your knees bent and wear a back-supporting belt.
- Avoid sleeping on your stomach.
- Attention to posture and lifting motion is beneficial.
- Men who carry their wallet in their back pocket should get it out of there and sit without being thrown off balance by sitting on their money.
- A cold pack made by wrapping crushed ice in a towel should be applied to the injured area for 20 minutes on and 20 minutes off at the first sign of injury. After the initial inflammation is reduced, you may then apply heat at night.
- Stretch for flexibility and to relax those aching muscles that support your back.
- Getting out of bed can be hazardous to your back. Turn on your side and roll.
- Take a look at your mattress. If it sags, you aren't doing your back a favour. Get a new one or put a board underneath so that the mattress can

give your back better support.
- Get out of your arm chair and into a rocking chair. The rocking motion appears to block nerve impulses that produce lower back pain. It also improves circulation and has a relaxing effect. American President J F Kennedy made the rocking chair treatment for a bad back very popular.
- Using a juicer or a blender, make a drink of potato and celery and drink at least 12 ounces daily.

BAD BREATH

Just how horrible is your breath? Do strangers back away when they are first introduced to you? Maybe it is your appearance and maybe it is your breath – but you will never really be sure which it is – until you are sure your breath is as sweet as possible.
- Avoid highly spiced foods – they can stay with you for as long as 24 hours.
- Coffee, beer, wine and whisky leave a residue, so avoid them as much as you can.
- Carry a toothbrush and use it immediately after you eat and be sure to brush your tongue as well because it is covered with little hair-like projections that trap food odours.
- Bad breath can also be caused by avoiding meals, so eat three meals a day.
- Eat parsley, a sure breath cleanser. It will also help to suck on a section of lemon at the end of a meal.
- Increase your intake of greens, as they contain natural chlorophyll.

BALDNESS

You spend more time worrying about your hair than you do about your job. You think about it all day long. Try as you might, nothing seems to cover that bald spot. You comb your hair over it and spray it down, but it seems to get shinier every day.

Ninety-nine per cent of hair loss (going from sparse to bald) is hereditary, but most of us never give up hope that it is only imagination, particularly when we become aware of all that hair on our hair brush. Take a look at your mother's hair: if her hair is thinning, the likelihood is that your hair will too.

Everyone normally loses between 50 to 100 hairs daily. As hair falls out, new hair grows in. Hair goes through a natural cycle of growth and rest.

However, factors such as diet, medications, natural hormones, improper hair care and certain diseases can also cause hair loss. It is best to have the underlying cause pinpointed before deciding baldness is inevitable.

Here are some folk remedies that have lasted for centuries because they seem to be effective:

- Lie down on a slanted board for 15 minutes daily to allow the blood to reach the scalp.
- Rub sesame oil into your scalp at bedtime and cover with a sleep cap to keep it off the pillowcase. In the morning wash with a mild shampoo and rinse with a mixture of 1 tablespoonful of apple cider vinegar in warm water.
- Press several cloves of garlic and massage the oil into your scalp, cover with a sleep cap. And – you better wash it off in the morning if you want anyone to sit next to you at work!
- Mix alcohol and cayenne pepper and rub into the scalp. You should feel very warm as this mixture is thought to stimulate the blood supply to the hair follicles.

If you choose to wear a hairpiece, be sure that it matches your natural colour and fits properly. Then keep it clean and groomed.

BEDWETTING

Most children are terribly embarrassed by bedwetting and it can create a major trauma if they are asked to stay overnight at someone else's house. They will grow out of it, but until they do:

- Don't praise and don't punish. Usually the problem will just go away as the child gets older.
- Make it possible for the child to change the sheets himself. Put out dry bedding and dry pyjamas. This will help the child to feel less babyish.
- Practise using the bladder muscles during the daytime. Have the child drink lots of fluids and then practise bladder control by holding off from going to the bathroom for as long as possible without having an accident.
- Children outgrow bedwetting at the rate of 15 per cent a year, so be patient.

BELCHING

Some societies think belching is good for you – but if you don't live in Calcutta and you cannot control your belching, then it is time to do something about it.

- Begin by being aware of air swallowing. People who belch a lot swallow air along with their food.
- Avoid carbonated beverages.
- Eat slowly and chew your food.
- Eat with your mouth closed.
- Do not use chewing gum.
- Decrease your intake of gassy foods, particularly those which include fats and oils, such as sour cream, salad oil and margarine, and those you know produce gas, such as Brussels sprouts.

BENIGN BREAST LUMPS

You rub soapy hands over yourself in the shower and suddenly, you feel something that wasn't there before. Your first thought is, "breast cancer!", but wait, maybe it isn't.

If you find a lump in your breast, more than likely it is completely harmless and due to a condition called fibrocystic breast disease. This is not actually a disease but a condition resulting from a woman's monthly hormone cycles during the childbearing years. Diet can also affect the formation of these lumps and nodules.

Benign lumps need expert examination but benign breast conditions have certain characteristics:

Benign lumps have a definable outline and can be easily moved within the breast. These lumps feel tender and are most noticeable before menstruation.

- Buy a special bra. Professionally fitted for daytime (and possibly a sleeping bra) may make you more comfortable.
- Reduce caffeine use. Many women report dramatic relief after eliminating coffee, tea, colas, chocolate.
- Curb salt intake. Limiting salt 10 days before your menstrual period may reduce swelling.
- Vitamin E (400 International Units [IU] daily). Some women find that pain and lumpiness is dramatically reduced with vitamin E supplementation.

BLACK EYE

Nobody believes that old, 'I walked into a door' story anymore, but however you got that black eye, you want to get rid of it as soon as possible.

- Apply an ice pack for the first 24 to 48 hours. Use crushed ice for 10 minutes every 2 hours.
- Avoid aspirin: it is an anticoagulant and you may find you have a worse black eye than you started out with. Instead, use acetaminophen for the pain.
- Don't blow your nose, as it can increase the swelling and the chance of an infection.
- Use some concealer for the week that it takes for the eye to recover.

BLADDER INFECTIONS

You need to go to the bathroom every ten minutes and once you go, you have pain and burning as you urinate. It is laughingly known as 'honeymoon disease' because it frequently occurs with increased sexual activity – but sufferers don't think bladder infections are so funny.

Urinary tract infections are common – so common that most of us will have at least one sometime in our lives. The classic symptom of a bladder or urinary tract infection is difficulty in urinating or a painful sensation when you urinate. Even when you feel the urge, you release only a small amount and the urge quickly returns.

The most common cause of bladder infections is the E coli bacterium. It resides in your intestinal tract and may migrate through your lymph system to your bladder. Urinary tract infections are more common among women; the short distance between the anus and vagina, the short length of the urethra, make women more prone to them than men.

- Wipe from front to back. Correct hygiene when using the toilet can keep infectious bacteria from coming into contact with your urethra.
- Empty your bladder often. Do this as soon as you feel the need to urinate. Women who are most prone to recurring infections tend to be 'holders'.
- Drink plenty of liquids. Fluids (6 to 8 glasses daily) can dilute your urine and help avoid stagnation of urine.
- If you use a diaphragm it can press against your urethra and prevent your bladder from emptying completely. Remove the diaphragm at the recommended time after intercourse.

- Hot sitz baths with 1 cupful of vinegar added to the water twice daily for 10 to 20 minutes will relieve the pain of cystitis.
- Cranberry juice capsules will prevent the bacteria from adhering to the bladder wall and will avoid the usual 30 per cent sugar content of most cranberry juices. Taken regularly they will keep the bladder healthy.
- Women should empty the bladder both soon before and soon after intercourse.
- Keep the genital and anal areas clean and dry.
- Avoid citrus fruits; they produce alkaline urine that encourages bacterial growth.
- Avoid caffeine, carbonated beverages, coffee, chocolate and alcohol.
- Include plenty of celery, parsley and water-melon in your diet – they act as natural diuretics.

BLISTERS

A blister is a message from your body – ouch! Those new shoes are just too tight.

- Protect a tender blister by placing a moleskin doughnut over the blister.
- Do not prick or drain a blister, it is protecting the tender spot underneath.
- Once the blister has drained, do not take the skin off the top of it: this is Nature's bandage.
- Experts suggest that you cover the blister during the day and then let it air at night.
- Once the blister has begun to heal, keep the area soft and moist with some vitamin E oil or aloe vera gel.
- The best course is to avoid blisters in the first place. Always wear socks and powder on the inside of your shoes to help the socks glide inside the shoes.

BODY ODOUR

We all know that we smell like a rose garden, so any recommendations in this item are for other people (those you just stood next to in the lift), of course.

Each individual has their own body odour and it is related to both their pheremones and genetics. However, some body odours are excessively offensive.

Both medication and diet can contribute to unpleasant body odours, as well as some disease processes.

- Bathing regularly and changing clothing frequently should diminish body odour.
- Natural fabrics such as cotton absorb perspiration better than synthetics.
- A small amount of white vinegar over the sweat glands under the arms and on the feet will decrease body odour.
- A change of diet can be effective. It is known that meat eaters have a heavier body odour than vegetarians, so consider changing or limiting the amount of meat in your diet. Spices, fish curry and garlic are excreted through the sweat glands of your body and keep you odoriferous for many hours after you've already forgotten you ate them.
- Baking soda dusted under the arms can keep the armpits smelling sweet.
- Increase your intake of chlorophyll (contained in all green foods).
- A combination of zinc, magnesium, para-aminobenzoic acid and vitamin B can combat offensive body odour.
- If you have tried everything, bathe in tomato juice by adding it to your bath water. It is known to work on dogs who have been sprayed by a skunk!

BOILS

A volcano erupts on your skin! And you tend to get these ugly, red, painful boils frequently. Boils are tender, pus-filled, raised areas of skin. Staphylococcus bacteria invade a break in the skin and infect a blocked oil gland or hair follicle. A carbuncle occurs when the infection spreads and additional boils appear. The formation of carbuncles indicates that the immune system is depressed.

Boils usually appear suddenly and within 24 hours become red and pus-filled. Swelling of the lymph gland closest to the boil may occur. Boils most often appear on the scalp, buttocks, face, neck and underarms.

- The infected area should be washed several times daily and an antiseptic applied to the area.
- A warm moist compress applied several times daily is the very best thing you can do for a boil. This will encourage the boil to come to a head, drain and heal.
- Honey mixed with vitamin E oil applied directly to the infected area will speed an immune response.
- If the boil is rubbed by clothing, you can speed its removal by sterilising

a glass bottle, then inverting the bottle and inserting a lighted match. The flame will use up all the oxygen in the bottle – immediately place the bottle over the boil, holding it tightly to the surrounding skin. The vacuum created will pull the infectious material out of the boil and immediately relieve the pain.

- Once the boil has broken, disinfect the area with a mixture of water and hydrogen peroxide.
- If you are prone to boils, increased hygiene will aid in removing the surface bacteria on the skin.
- Ten capsules of odourless garlic taken over the day will act as a natural antibiotic.

BREAST-FEEDING

Breast-feeding does great things for both babies and mothers. Some hints can make it trouble-free.

- Choose a good nursing bra. Choose all cotton. Make sure you can open and close the bra with one hand.
- Position the baby correctly. Tickle the baby's lower lip with your nipple so that the baby will open wide. The nipple needs to be inserted deep into the baby's throat so that the baby can suck properly.
- Nurse from both breasts during each feeding and nurse often. This creates a better bonding between mother and baby.
- Don't toughen the nipples. If baby is positioned correctly this won't be necessary.
- Do not use soap on the nipples, as this dries them out. Glands around the areola produce oil with an antiseptic in it so soap is unnecessary. Then air-dry the nipples before covering them.
- Use your own milk to help heal sore nipples. Express a little of the milk and rub it around the nipple. This milk is high in lubricants and contains an antibiotic.
- Control leakage by pressing against the nipple with the heel of your hand.

BRONCHITIS

The coughing is exhausting. You feel as if it comes all the way from your toes; it keeps you from sleeping and you are worn out. You have bronchitis.

Bronchitis is inflammation of the upper breathing tubes that lead to the lungs.

This inflammation creates irritation which causes constant coughing, a build-up of mucus, accompanied by fever, back and chest pain, a sore throat and difficulty in breathing.

Acute bronchitis is the result of an upper respiratory tract infection and often ends up in pneumonia.

Chronic bronchitis is frequent irritation of the airways but is not an infection. Often this chronic condition is caused by allergies.

- Stop smoking. This is the most important thing you can do.
- If an allergy is the cause then the allergen should be pinpointed and avoided, if possible.
- Drink plenty of fluids to loosen mucus.
- Add moisture to the air to ease breathing. Eucalyptus oil added to a vaporiser can aid in the relief of symptoms.

BRUISING

How many times have you walked into the edge of that darn coffee table? Unless you just stay in bed every day, you are bound to bruise yourself from time to time.

When underlying tissue is damaged without breaking the skin, black and blue marks will result because blood collects underneath the skin.

- As soon as possible, apply an ice pack to constrict the ruptured ends of the tiny blood vessels in the area. Remove after 20 minutes, allow the area to rewarm and then reapply the ice pack.
- After 24 hours, use heat to dilate the blood vessels and improve circulation to the area.
- Add 500 mg vitamin C to your daily diet and you will be less prone to bruising when you do have an occasional bump. Oranges and grapefruits are good sources.
- Avoid excessive aspirin.
- Grate a turnip, apply it to the bruise for 15 to 30 minutes after the ice. It is thought that this will speed up the removal of the blood from the area.
- You can also bind the inside of a banana peel to the area to reduce the pain and lessen the probability of discoloration. A banana peel over the eye will do a better job of lessening the discoloration than the proverbial steak.

BRUXISM

Instead of sleeping peacefully, you are grinding and gritting your poor teeth together, sometimes all night long. You wake up with a sore jaw and very sensitive teeth.

Bruxism is thought to be a reaction to stress or anger. It can result in loosening of the teeth and recession of the gums, headaches and sometimes TMJ (temporomandibular joint syndrome).

- An athlete's mouthguard can be purchased in a sporting goods store and placed in the mouth for a few nights to break the habit.
- Eat something like an apple or carrot just before bedtime to tire the jaw muscles.
- Additional calcium such as 8 ounces of milk, taken before bedtime, has been shown to aid in the relaxation of the jaw muscles and can be effective in just a few days.
- If possible, reduce stress and make bedtime more relaxing.
- Avoid evening caffeine and refined carbohydrates.
- Avoid exciting television viewing or much activity prior to sleep.
- Relax with a warm bath just before bedtime.

BURNS

You touch the iron, you get steam in your face when you take the lid off a saucepan, you splash some grease on yourself when cooking breakfast. It is easy to burn yourself occasionally.

- Stop the burning process – flush the burn with lots of cold water.
- Cold water and lots of it, not ice, should be applied, by pouring water over the burned area.
  - □ Prompt cooling can halt the progression of any burn and can prevent damage to the deeper layer of skin.
  - □ First degree: Skin is reddened.
  - □ Second degree: Skin is reddened with blistering.
  - □ Third degree: Entire thickness of the skin and the underlying muscle has been destroyed.
  - □ Third degree burns need immediate professional attention.
- Second and third degree burns can be treated, after cooling, by applying honey under a dry dressing. It is a cleansing and healing agent.
- Do not apply butter or ointments and do not break the blisters, as those

bubbles of raised skin are Nature's own best bandage. Watch the burn closely for any sign of infection as open areas of the skin are prime targets.

- Aloe vera is excellent after healing has begun. Vitamin E applied when healing has begun may prevent scarring.

BURSITIS

Your shoulder or elbow hurts every time you move or lift something, sometimes even as light as a pencil. You've heard of 'tennis elbow' but you don't play the game. Bursitis often affects the hip or shoulder joints and although it is sometimes called tennis elbow or frozen shoulder it can affect any joint.

Bursae are little fluid-filled sacs which ensure the smooth, frictionless working of the body's many joints. Not until you have a problem with one of them are you even aware they exist. Bursitis is an inflammation of these small fluid-filled sacs which aid in the movement of muscles and protect and cushion the bones against friction. This kind of inflammation can be caused by injury, ingredients in foods, allergy and calcium deposits.

The joint can be tender to touch and acute pain in the region will cause you to limit motion of the joint.

- During the initial phase of the injury, movement should be avoided as this will only increase both the inflammation and the pain.
- Rest is best and a sling is good for shoulder and elbows.
- Cold icepacks will reduce swelling and pain.

Once the acute period of pain and swelling is over, movement becomes essential to return the joint to normal.

- Apply caster oil over the joint, cover with a dressing and then apply a heating pad.
- Continued immobility can cause adhesions which will result in a permanent condition. After a few days, stretching is recommended.
- Avoid overdoing any repetitive motion. Individuals who play sports, such as tennis, need to get some help in correcting their style of playing to avoid further injury.

CARPAL TUNNEL SYNDROME

If you have to stop writing a short letter, or put down the broom in the middle of sweeping up because of pain in the wrist and hand, and you awaken in the morning with a numbness that you cannot understand, it just might be carpal tunnel syndrome.

Cumulative trauma caused by repeated movements of the hands and wrists is usually the cause. As computers become available to everyone, carpal tunnel syndrome seems to be on the rise everywhere.

- 2 mg daily of vitamin B6 seems to be beneficial – but be ready to wait for 12 weeks or more before you see any improvement. Do not exceed this dosage, as B6 is toxic at high dosages.
- While you are waiting for the B6 to do its work, begin some gentle exercise for the hands and wrists. Rotate the hands around in gentle circles to stimulate circulation to the injured area. Raise your arms above your head and rotate both the arm and the wrist. This improves the circulation to the shoulder, neck and upper back.
- Take a break. If you are working long hours at any task, take a few minutes away from the work and turn your head and shrug your shoulders.
- Use ice for 20 minutes at a time to decrease the inflammation.

CAT ALLERGY

You love that kitty-cat, you love to hold it on your lap and listen to the gentle purring as you stroke the soft fur.

The cat lover is often dismayed to find that the cause of those runny eyes and itchy, watery nose is none other than their beloved pet. Cat allergy comes from a cat's oil-producing glands in its skin and its saliva. When cat dander gets airborne, an allergenic individual can have a reaction without even touching the cat.

An allergy is a mistaken activation of your immune system. This system makes antibodies to protect your body from invaders.

- The obvious answer, of course, is to avoid cats completely.
- If you find a new home for your cat, thoroughly clean the house. It can take months for the allergens to disappear from the carpeting and furniture.

However, most cat lovers wouldn't dream of removing kitty from membership of the household. So, if you do decide to keep your cat you must reduce the allergens.

- Wash the cat once a week in distilled water. This will reduce the amount of airborne allergens by 90 per cent.
- Minimise carpeting and upholstered furniture.
- Use an effective air cleaner. Air cleaners will remove more than 99 per

cent of dust particles that pass through them.
- Control the cat's access to some of the rooms within the home. Most importantly, keep the cat out of the bedroom.
- After petting your cat, wash your hands thoroughly before you touch your face and nose.

CATARACTS

Objects may appear clouded or maybe you see halos around lights or are troubled by glare. As you age, the lens of your eye becomes progressively opaque.
- Research indicates that lack of vitamin B2 (riboflavin) may be responsible for cataracts. Try taking 1 tablespoonful a day of Brewer's yeast.
- Drop 2 drops of castor oil into each eye at bedtime. Continue the treatment for a month and see if you find it is dissolving the cataract before opting for surgery.
- Time is on your side. While a cataract can increasingly cloud the lens, it rarely damages other eye structures.

CAVITIES

Most of us are terrified just thinking about a visit to the dentist – but putting it off or neglecting your teeth can create serious dental troubles.

Routine daily dental care can minimise problems and help you stay out of the dentist's surgery, except for routine cleaning sessions.

Plaque is a sticky, bacteria-containing solution that clings to the surface of your teeth and, unless it is removed every 24 hours, can harden into tartar. Hardened tartar at the gum line irritates the gums so that they pull away from the base of the tooth and set the mouth up for gum disease.
- Daily flossing and brushing is a must.
- Sticky, chewy foods, such as dried fruits and honey are examples of foods that can create difficulties by clinging to the surface of the teeth. These foods create acids that erode tooth enamel.
- If you must eat sweets, eat them with other foods to buffer their effects on your teeth.
- Snack on foods which will actually work to remove plaque as well as sugar acids, such as carrots or celery.
- A fluoride toothpaste will aid in preventing cavities.
- Don't use your teeth as tools, such as for opening hair pins.

CELLULITE

Those ugly puckers! That orange peel-looking skin on the thighs and buttocks! Nobody wants it but everybody seems to have some, no matter how thin. Most experts disagree about exactly what it is but everyone agrees that they'd like to get rid of it.

Some say it is no more than pockets of fat and its appearance is due to strands of fibrous tissue anchored to the skin. Some non-medical people say it is a combination of fat globules, waste matter, and water in connective tissue.

- Exercise and attempt to keep your weight at normal levels.
- Eat plenty of fresh fruit and vegetables and drink fruit and vegetable juices.
- Relax in a home mineral bath containing sea salt. Use a loofah mitt to rub the trouble spots while you soak.
- Combat constipation and drink LOTS OF WATER. Avoid intake of salt which contributes to fluid retention.
- Avoid coffee and cigarettes as they constrict the blood vessels and make it more difficult to rid yourself of waste products.
- Massage those thighs with a kneading motion with hands that are moist with a mixture of witch-hazel and massage oils.

CERVICAL SMEAR TESTS

Cervical smear tests examine cells scraped from the cervix for abnormal changes.

- Annual cervical smear tests are recommended for all women. To ensure that the results are accurate, do not douche, use vaginal medications or inserts or have sexual intercourse for 24 hours before your test.
- You should not miss your test if you:
  - ☐ Became sexually active before age 18.
  - ☐ Have multiple sexual partners.
  - ☐ Have a history of pelvic infections.
  - ☐ Have had a previous abnormal test.

CHAFING

Something is rubbing you the wrong way and you don't like it at all. Collars rub on the back of your neck, your thighs rub together when you walk.

Not only does chafing leave you with painful skin, these abrasions increase the likelihood of an infection because they create a break in the skin, so they should not be treated lightly.

- Change to 100 per cent cotton clothing, particularly if you have extremely sensitive skin.
- If some fabric chafes, even after the first washing, get rid of it.
- Petroleum jelly or talcum powder between your thighs, under your arms, any place that chafing is troublesome, will lubricate the area and make fabrics glide over the area.
- If chafing has resulted from some particular exercise such as running, change your activity until the area heals.

CHAPPED HANDS

Oh, those painful and workworn-looking hands. Those knuckles that crack and bleed whenever you bend your fingers. Red, dry and cracked, very painful and very unattractive. It is best to avoid getting chapped hands in the first place rather than trying to hide them after they are chapped.

Low humidity in the autumn and winter dries and irritates the skin. Repeated washing removes the natural oil layer and allows moisture within the skin to evaporate.

- Begin by trying to wash only the palms of your hands or use an oil-free skin cleanser which doesn't require water to cleanse.
- After each handwash and at night before retiring, use a topical hand lotion.
- When working in the kitchen, use vegetable oil on your hands as soon as you are finished with the dishes.
- Keep your hands out of very hot water.
- Use gloves when working around the house or in the garden and always wear gloves outside in the winter time.
- Treat your hands to an oatmeal sloughing regime. Blend 1 cupful of uncooked old-fashioned rolled oats to a very fine powder. Rub over your hands; this will remove the dry skin. Rinse in cool water, pat dry and lavish with lots of vegetable oil or hand cream.

CHAPPED LIPS

You heard a great joke but you can't laugh because your lip will split. When your lips are chapped, sore and peeling it is difficult even to smile without pain.

- Avoid cold, dry weather with naked lips. Cover them with a lubricant before going outside.
- In the summer, cover them with a sunscreen so they don't get burned.
- A deficiency in B vitamins can contribute to cracks at the corners of the mouth, so keep your vitamins up.
- Moisturise your lips by drinking additional fluids in the winter.
- If you find you lick your lips a lot, be sure to carry lots of lip balm with you to replace that moisture.
- Some flavouring agents in toothpaste, chewing gum and mouthwash can cause chapped lips in some allergy-prone individuals. If this is the case, brush your teeth with baking soda only.

CHOLESTEROL

You are suffering from too much of a fatlike material in your blood and you didn't even know it until your doctor gave you the bad news. The higher the cholesterol level, the greater the risk of cardiovascular disease. This is a silent, painless process in which cholesterol-containing fatty deposits accumulate along the walls of the arteries. As the plaque builds up, the artery narrows and this reduces the flow of blood.

Dietary cholesterol is what is contained in the foods we eat. Serum cholesterol is what is in your blood stream and you want to keep that below a reading of 200. HDL (high density lipoprotein) cholesterol is the good part of cholesterol and it cleans up the arteries. LDL (low density lipoprotein) cholesterol is the bad guy and it clogs up the arteries.

So let's lower the serum cholesterol.

- Watch your weight because the more overweight you are, the more cholesterol you manufacture.
- Cut out the saturated fats in your diet.
- Eat lots of beans as they contain a water-soluble fibre called pectin that grabs the cholesterol and throws it out.
- Eat more fruit, another pectin product.
- Oat bran has got lots of good publicity as a cholesterol fighter but other grains which contain soluble fibre are just as good at the job.
- Exercise. This raises your levels of HDL and lowers LDL.
- Take garlic capsules – they are excellent in reducing blood fats.
- Reduce your intake of coffee, cigarettes and other artery narrowers and try to relax more. Relaxation has been shown to reduce cholesterol levels.

COLD SORES

It's going to be a fever blister – just when you were going to have your picture taken. That tingling on your lip lets you know that you can expect one to blossom forth in the next day or so.

The herpes simplex virus is the cause of this problem and if you know someone who hasn't had one by the time they are an adult, they have probably built up an immunity long ago. Lucky them.

- Keep cold sores clean and dry.
- Get yourself a new toothbrush right away as the old one probably has enough of the virus living in it to continue to reinfect you.
- Protect the lesion with petroleum jelly – but use a cotton wool bud to get it out of the jar, not your finger.
- A water-based zinc solution, applied as soon as you feel that initial tingle may help speed the healing.
- Increase your intake of the amino acid lysine which can be found in dairy products, potatoes and Brewer's yeast.
- Avoid foods rich in arginine as the virus needs that amino acid to grow. Arginine is found in chocolate, cola drinks, peas, grain cereals, various nuts and beer.
- Protect your lips from sun and wind as soon as you feel that first tingle.
- Try to reduce stress as it appears to cause the blisters to appear.
- Gentle exercise is beneficial in reducing stress.

COLIC

The baby never seems to stop crying. One mother said, "That baby cries 25 hours out of each 24." A crying baby who pulls their knees up to their belly and seems to be in real pain probably has colic. Nothing seems to help, not changing the nappy or feeding or holding and rocking. But, take hope, most babies grow out of colic by the third or fourth month.

Some colicky babies are more gassy and may be more difficult to burp.

- If bottle-feeding, burp after every ounce.
- Hold the baby upright when feeding and try some different teats on the bottle.
- A milk-free diet for the mother who is breast-feeding is well worth a try. Other things in the mother's diet that are thought to contribute are carbonated drinks, chocolate, bananas, strawberries and spicy foods.

- Wrapping in a 'mummy wrap' and holding the colicky baby seems to help too.
- Turn on the vacuum cleaner and leave it running. Some mothers swear by this humming sound treatment.
- Place a heating pad set on low on the baby's abdomen.
- A swing seat or being held by mother in a rocking chair can also be useful as it has a calming effect on babies.

COMMON COLD

Everybody gets them and nobody wants them. There is still no cure for the common cold, even though we can put men in orbit and walk on the moon.

The sneezing, the runny nose, the headachy feeling, a common or garden variety of cold can keep you home from work – but there are some things you can do to make getting through the week, which is the time a cold usually lasts, a little more comfortable.

- Take vitamin C, found in oranges and grapefruit; it is an excellent antioxidant.
- Suck on zinc lozenges at the very first sign of a cold. Zinc changes the acid balance of the climate in the nose and throat, where cold bugs prefer to get a foothold, and makes it more difficult for them to do so.
- Rest and relax. Take some time for yourself, just watch television, read and sleep for a few hours. You'll feel better and you'll get better sooner – and you won't be spreading your cold germs to everyone at work.
- It is now an accepted scientific fact that chicken soup can help unclog that stuffy nose.
- Drink at least 8 glasses of water, juice or other clear liquid each day.
- Smoking will aggravate a throat that is already raspy, so this is as good a time to kick the habit as any.
- A warm salt water gargle will help you feel better too.
- Take a steamy shower to clear up the congestion and then bundle up and get into bed before you get chilled.
- If your nose is sore from blowing and wiping, put some petroleum jelly both inside and out.
- Throw used tissues away and wash your hands before you touch your face again so you don't reinfect yourself and your family.

CONSTIPATION

Everyone gets constipated occasionally. You get busy running around, staying out late, paying very little attention to your diet, eating meals on the run – and suddenly you are constipated.

When you realise you have the problem, the first thing to do is:

- Take a look at your fluid intake and increase it.
- Add dietary fibre immediately. From 25 to 35 grams daily for all adults, from complex carbohydrates such as whole grains, fruits and vegetables. Fibre supplements are available from your pharmacist and they promote regularity about the same way fibre in foods do.
- Prunes are a good natural laxative, as well as a good snack.
- Exercise increases the rate by which food travels through your digestive system.
- Walking is particularly helpful.
- Do not ignore the urge – try to toilet-train yourself again.
- Tension and anxiety can cause constipation because this is part of the fight-or-flight syndrome. Try to relax and calm down.
- Some foods are constipating. Everyone knows the expression 'it makes the cheese more binding', and for some, all dairy products have the same effect.
- If you are really uncomfortable, an occasional enema or a suppository will be OK, but remember laxatives can become addicting very easily. It is much better to rely on fibre and fluids to regulate yourself.

CORNS AND CALLUSES

Corns and calluses aren't just a nuisance. They have a purpose – to protect your skin. These extra layers of firm, thick tissue develop where toughened skin resists constant friction, particularly over bony prominences or at the site of repeated trauma. But this protection can be a problem if the growth becomes large, inflamed or painful.

Calluses can develop on your heel or the bottom of your foot. You can get calluses on your hands from repeated labour, from using hand tools. They often occur on a person whose occupation entails repeated injury to a particular area, such as the knees of gardeners and the ankles of ice-skaters.

Corns are smaller than calluses. Hard corns may occur on the tops or sides of your toes. Soft corns develop between your toes.

- Wear comfortable shoes. Ill-fitting footwear often is the main cause of corns and calluses. Wear shoes that don't cramp your toes. The addition of soft insoles will aid in cushioning your feet.
- Adjust your walking style. An improper gait, such as walking on the sides of your feet, can produce corns and calluses. Look at the heels on an old pair of shoes. If one side is markedly worn, a shoe insert could help distribute your weight more evenly.
- Safeguard your skin. You can find a wide variety of readily available, inexpensive products such as lamb's wool, moleskin pads and toe coverings to protect your skin.
- Toughen thin skin. Gently rub with a pumice stone after bathing. The alkalinity of soap, along with the soaking in water, softens your skin so you can rub off the upper layers. Don't try to remove all the toughened skin at once; this process may take several weeks.
- Don't trim a corn or callus, especially if you have diabetes or circulation problems – you might introduce an infection.
- Place either pure papaya juice or a piece of papaya pulp on a cotton pad and bind in place directly on the corn. Leave this treatment on overnight and change the cotton pad daily.

CUTS, SCRAPES AND PUNCTURE WOUNDS

We all get a minor injury, a paper cut or a little scrape on our skin now and then. React swiftly and apply gentle pressure. Press down on the cut using a clean soft cloth. (Cuts that gape open, bleed profusely or have jagged edges need medical attention.)

- Clean any cut with mild soap and warm water. Flushing the wound under running water helps remove debris and bacteria.
- A small cut can be treated with the application of honey which contains enzymes which aid in healing.
- Peel a banana and apply the inside of the peel directly on the small injury and secure it firmly against the injury. Change the peel every three or four hours for a rapid healing treatment. After 24 hours remove any peel and expose the injury to air. Exposing the wound to air will further speed this healing process.
- Wash puncture wounds and call your doctor. Puncture wounds are deceiving: they may look small, but the object causing the wound (nail, scissors, etc) may carry germs deep into your body.

- Keep your tetanus booster up to date. Adults need a booster every 10 years. If you suffer a deep puncture wound, you may need an additional booster shot at the time of injury.
- Be alert to infection. A cut or scrape that becomes sore, red or contains pus is infected. See your doctor.

CYSTITIS

You are running to the bathroom every 10 minutes and now you see that your urine is bloody. Cystitis is an uncomfortable bladder infection, accompanied by the need to urinate frequently, together with pain and burning.

The most common cause is the bacteria E coli (causing up to 85 per cent of urinary tract infections). This is present in the colon of every individual and is part of the process of digestion. It causes trouble when it reaches the opening into the bladder, and is the reason that care should be taken at bowel movements to cleanse properly so as not to transmit this bacteria to the bladder.

Women are 10 times more likely than men to acquire bladder infections because of the closeness of the urethra to the anus.

- Do not delay urination more than two or three hours.
- Drink lots of fluids, which increase hydration and cause the bacteria to be flushed out of the bladder.
- Avoid caffeinated and carbonated drinks, alcohol and diet soda which can further irritate the bladder.
- Drink diluted cranberry juice, as it contains a chemical known as hippuric acid that keeps the bacteria from clinging to the bladder wall.
- Reduce acidic fruits, vegetables and spicy foods.
- Drink a full glass of water before and after sex and empty bladder immediately after sex if you are prone to these infections.
- Add one small box of baking soda to a bath of warm water, sit in it for approximately 30 minutes and then rinse.
- Include garlic in your diet as it is a natural antibiotic. Odour-free garlic capsules can be taken throughout the day until symptoms are resolved.
- If you take antibiotics prescribed by a doctor, add yoghurt with active cultures to your diet, during and after the course of antibiotics, to replace the healthy bacteria your body needs.

Bladder infections in men may be a sign of a more serious problem, such as prostatitis.

DANDRUFF

Your head itches and you scratch, even though you know you are going to loosen lots of white flakes to drift down onto the shoulders of your black suit. Everyone has been embarrassed at one time or another by that snowstorm from the scalp.

The cells of the scalp turn over, just as all other areas of the skin. This is a natural and normal occurrence. When the process of shedding these cells increases, the shedding becomes noticeable. Sometimes these shedding scalp cells cause itching which causes the person to scratch, loosening more scales and increasing the visibility of the dandruff.

Hormonal changes, excessive shampooing or changes in the weather have all been blamed for dandruff. Acute emotional distress and unrelieved anxiety can also contribute to the condition.

- Relieve the stress and anxiety in your life. Simple dandruff may be a signal from your body that you need to slow down and get more rest.
- Avoid fried foods, dairy products, sugar, chocolate and nuts, which contribute to the greasy condition of the scalp, the forerunner of dandruff.
- Begin by applying the undiluted juice of several lemons directly to the scalp. Wash the hair and scalp with a mild shampoo, such as one recommended for babies, and then rinse thoroughly. Follow this rinse with another made from a mixture of lemon juice and water. Repeat this treatment daily until the dandruff is gone.

DENTURES

You have to give up your favourite, blackberry pie.

Wobbly dentures are a reason to avoid a variety of foods we usually enjoy, such as apples or berries. If your dentures hurt or feel loose, the problem may be either that they don't fit correctly, or improper care.

- Ask your dentist to check your dentures and be sure they fit the current shape of your mouth. If they fit well, you shouldn't need an adhesive preparation. If they don't fit, they may need adjustment. When your natural teeth were lost or removed, the jaw bone that supported them began to shrink. Well-fitting dentures may eventually become loose. Taking good care of your dentures will help keep them comfortable and durable.
- Remove dentures each night to give your gums a rest.
- To prevent distortion, store your dentures in water. Do not soak dentures

with a metal base for more than 15 minutes in a cleaning solution.
- Clean your dentures daily to remove trapped food particles.
- Brush and floss any remaining teeth, and massage your gums daily with a brush, a cloth or a clean finger, to keep them healthy and firm.

DEPRESSION

Everyone goes through times when they just feel 'down in the mouth'. Usually these times are self-limiting and in a few weeks we just seem to feel better without thinking anything has really changed in our lives.

True depression is characterised by feelings of loss of self-esteem and despondency, often described as different from normal unhappiness. Early waking, loss of appetite (or greatly increased appetite), weight loss or gain, and diminished libido are common.

The neurotransmitters which regulate mood and behaviour are dopamine, serotonin and norepinephrine. When the brain produces serotonin, you feel more relaxed. When it produces dopamine or norepinephrine, you think and act more quickly and are generally more alert.

Fats inhibit the ability of our bodies to utilise these neurotransmitters because they cause the blood cells to clump and become sticky, resulting in poor circulation to the brain.
- Whenever you feel sad or blue, begin by limiting your intake of fats.
- Excessive sugar is implicated in depression because it causes a spurt of energy and then the 'sugar blues' when that spurt of energy is followed by extreme fatigue, so avoid giving yourself a sweet treat in an effort to feel more cheery.
- Caffeine, cigarettes and alcohol also contribute to nervous energy and depression, as well as highs and lows of mood.
- A proper diet is absolutely essential. Add two bananas to your diet, as they contain serotonin and norepinephrine, those natural mood elevators which can ease the level of bad feelings.
- Complex carbohydrates, such as vegetables and pastas raise the level of tryptophan in the brain, which is calming.
- Add lots of oregano and celery to salads for their calming effects.
- An Epsom salts bath while sipping a cup of camomile tea for 30 minutes of tension-free relaxation is an excellent benefit.
- For those cases of continuing depression which are not lifted in a few weeks, professional assistance should be sought.

DIABETES

You've been diagnosed with diabetes and told you must keep your blood sugar under control. That isn't the end of all the fun in your life, since you can virtually eliminate all the symptoms of diabetes by following a regimen of nutrition, weight control and exercise.

- Start with the Diabetic Association's diet, tailored to fit your individual needs.
- Eat small meals and eat more frequently.
- Avoid alcohol but if you should have a drink, exchange alcohol calories for fat calories.
- Avoid omega-3 supplements, as they increase blood glucose levels.
- Maintain a proper weight for your height.
- Involve your family in helping you make and keep those nutritional changes and improved eating habits.
- Exercise, as it increases the number of insulin receptors. Try walking; it is the best exercise for a diabetic.
- Take proper care of your teeth, because diabetics are more prone to infections.
- Take proper care of your feet. Nerve damage lessens the ability to experience pain, so a little sore unnoticed can develop into something more serious.
- Reduce stress: it affects blood sugar levels and makes it harder to adhere to your routine.
- Test your blood rather than your urine. Urine must have high levels of glucose before it is apparent that you are in difficulty.
- Read the label on over-the-counter medications, because many of them are not for use by diabetics.
- Avoid aspirin and caffeine. Aspirin lowers blood sugar levels and caffeine raises it.

DIARRHOEA

The curtain just went up on the play you spent a week's wages to buy tickets to see and suddenly you are struck with abdominal cramping and a sweaty feeling. Everyone dreads a bout of diarrhoea, which can leave you feeling exhausted and dehydrated.

After you eat, most foods are digested in the small intestine. Your colon then absorbs the remaining liquid from digested food particles that pass through it, forming semi-solid stools.

Your system can become imbalanced in two ways:

1. Bacteria, commonly found in food or water that is contaminated, can make a toxin that triggers intestinal cells to secrete salt and water. When this occurs, it overwhelms the capacity of your lower small bowel and your colon to absorb fluid.

2. More commonly, an invading virus can damage the mucous membrane that lines the intestine. Fluid absorption is then disrupted.

- At the first sign of diarrhoea, begin to drink clear liquids – the main liquid you need is water. You might also include broth, teas of camomile or raspberry leaves, gelatin, ice-lollies and fruit drinks or juices (except prune).

- Drink lots of liquids – at least 8 to 10 glasses or water and other liquids daily. This should prevent most complications that stem from substantial loss of fluids and electrolytes such as sodium and potassium.

- Eat low-fibre foods. As the symptoms improve or stools become formed, start to eat low-fibre foods, such as crackers, toast, eggs, rice or chicken and other tender cuts of meat.

- Don't eat greasy or fatty foods, milk or highly seasoned foods for a few days.

- You need to replenish the friendly bacteria in your system. Drink several glasses of buttermilk or sauerkraut juice. You might also eat some pickled beets or sauerkraut as soon as you feel able to do so.

- Avoid over-the-counter anti-diarrhoea products. These may slow the elimination of the infectious agent and actually prolong the diarrhoea.

Short-term diarrhoea doesn't require any other treatment. Sometimes diarrhoea is a sign of a more serious illness or can lead to complications. See your doctor if the problem lasts longer than three days.

DIURETICS

Your feet are so swollen you can't get your shoes on and you feel like you swallowed a football.

Fluid retention can be a problem that results in a bloated feeling, swollen feet and ankles, particularly for pregnant women. Anyone taking a diuretic routinely is at risk of losing too much potassium from the body.

- Replace that potassium by eating several bananas daily, and try a natural diuretic, such as cucumber, celery or lettuce.

DIVERTICULOSIS

With age, your muscles can weaken and become less able to push waste along. Diverticulosis occurs when pouches, called diverticula, protrude through weak spots in your colon.

- Increase your fibre intake. Foods such as wheat bran, wholegrain products and fresh fruits and vegetables can help keep your stools soft and easier to pass.
- Increase fluids, drink at least 6 to 8 glasses of water a day.

If a pouch becomes inflamed or infected (a condition called *diverticulitis*), your doctor may recommend a low-fibre diet but only temporarily.

- Once the inflammation clears, slowly switch back to a high-fibre diet. It is no longer believed that seeds or other high-fibre particles lodge in pouches and cause inflammation.

DRY MOUTH

Just thinking about public speaking often causes a dry mouth. Words stick in your throat and your tongue seems to be glued to the roof of your mouth.

- Resist the temptation to drink very cold beverages: they will contribute to increasing an already tense throat.
- Avoid any liquids that contain dairy products, such as tea with milk: they increase mucus or phlegm and escalate the difficulties of talking.
- Opera singers for generations have used warm tea and honey to lubricate the mouth, warm the vocal cords, and create an oral environment that makes vocalising easy.
- If you really get stuck in the middle of an all-important speech, gently but subtly, chew on your own tongue. This chewing action will produce sufficient saliva to moisten your mouth within a few seconds.

DRY SKIN

Your face feels tight and tiny flakes of skin are visible at the corners of your nose. Your cheek feels like sandpaper and the rest of your body feels itchy.

- Dry skin is the result of lack of moisture.
- Avoid bathing more than once a day, alternate with a sponge bath.
- Use a very mild soap, avoid deodorant soap.
- Add bath oil to your bath water and remove make-up with a creamy

emolient rather than with soap.
- Pat dry instead of rubbing.
- Apply moisturiser while your skin is still damp, as this will lock in the surface moisture.
- Keep your hands out of hot water. Use gloves when doing any kind of work in water.
- Use a humidifier and keep the heat down low in the winter time, just enough to keep the chill out of the room. Wear warmer clothing rather than turning up the heat, which takes the moisture out of the air.

EARACHE

You feel feverish and your earlobe hurts when you brush your hand across it. You could have swimmer's ear. Most earaches occur in children, partially because their ear channel from the outside to the inner ear is straighter than that of adults and fluid which collects there cannot drain as easily. Persistent ear infections can cause eventual hearing loss.

The most common is known as swimmer's ear. Symptoms include slight fever, discharge from the ear, pain that is worse when the earlobe is touched and temporary loss of hearing in the ear.
- Treat minor earaches, such as those which are the result of a cold or the flu, by combining a few drops of onion juice with a teaspoonful of warm olive oil and place into the ear canal both morning and night. Keep the head to the side to allow the drops to get well into the ear and then plug the ear with cotton wool.
- If you swim in public pools, enquire about the treatment of the pool with chemicals before use.

EARWAX

Earwax's purpose is to lubricate the ear canal and trap bacteria, dust and other foreign substances which could enter the ear and cause problems. Occasionally, it accumulates in sufficient amounts to seriously interfere with hearing.
- It is not generally necessary to remove earwax. The ears should not be irrigated if you've had a perforated eardrum or mastoid surgery.
- If the ear is healthy and wax persists, loosen with a few drops of room temperature baby oil or mineral oil applied with an eyedropper. Do this

twice a day for several days.

- Warm a small amount of hydrogen peroxide, tilt the head to one side and drop the peroxide into the ear, allowing it to stay there while you hear a fizzing sound for three or four minutes and then gently remove with soft cotton.
- Do not use a cotton wool bud as this only serves to make the wax more compact and drive it deeper into the ear.
- A diet which is high in nutrition and low in fat, similar to that prescribed for heart patients, has been found to be beneficial for those with hearing loss that is not improved by the removal of earwax.

It may be that hearing loss and other ear symptoms may be forerunners of heart and artery disease and excessive wax formation may be associated with a high-fat diet.

EMPHYSEMA

Trying to breathe with emphysema feels like trying to breathe with a plastic bag over your face.

Emphysema is the loss of elasticity of the lung tissue. You can inhale but because of the loss of elasticity of the lung, you can't exhale the stale air. This stale air remains trapped in the lungs, preventing the intake of additional oxygen and the exhalation of carbon dioxide.

The symptoms of emphysema are breathlessness followed by coughing. Wheezing, recurrent respiratory infections and sometimes, weakness, weight loss and lack of libido may be some of the initial manifestations of the disease.

- A mild 'smoker's cough' is often present many years before the onset of difficulty in breathing upon exertion. The major factor in the progression of this disease is smoking. If you are smoking, you MUST stop. Smoking increases the rate of progression of this fatal disease.
- Prolonged inactivity can lead to excessive disability.

As long as there is no accompanying heart disease, it is essential that you maintain a regular exercise programme.

- Riding a stationary bicycle in a carefully monitored programme is beneficial, as the bicycle can be ridden in an air-controlled environment.
- A physical therapist can give instruction in proper breathing for those anxious individuals who develop excessively rapid ventilation during exertion.
- Avoid any air pollution. If this means changing your job, then do so.

- Avoid using any product in aerosol sprays.
- Avoid foods that lead to the formation of mucus, such as meat, eggs, dairy products and white flour.
- Avoid gas-forming foods such as beans – the gas can lead to abdominal distension which can interfere with breathing.
- Rest and avoid stress.
- Take nourishing soups and clear liquids. Foods that require a great deal of chewing make breathing while eating difficult.

ENDOMETRIOSIS

Your menstrual periods are very painful. Your lower back hurts for no apparent reason. Bowel movements and sexual intercourse are painful.

Endometrial tissue, which lines the inside of the uterus and is shed every month with the menstrual cycle has begun growing outside its proper place. Wherever it grows it forms a weblike scar along your other internal organs. In its new and improper location, it reacts to your hormones and swells and bleeds during menstruation, only it has no way to exit your body.

- Keep track of your menstrual cycle. Chart the things that seem to cause you pain and you can begin to recognise what they are and control them.
- Eat more fish as they contain omega-3 fatty acids which suppress prostaglandin production – one of the hormones that affect the lining of the uterus (endometrial tissue).
- Try bed rest, moist heat or a heating pad and warm drinks to relax the cramping caused by the uterine muscles.
- Exercise, as this reduces oestrogen levels and may slow the growth of the endometriosis.
- Reduce your intake of caffeine as this chemical increases your sensation of pain.
- Use a lubricant to ease painful intercourse.
- An accupressure technique that seems to help is to press the inside of your leg, approximately two inches above your ankle bone.

EXERCISE

We all know we should exercise regularly for good health and, while we are all filled with good intentions, it is very easy to find an excuse to avoid it.

The reasons most people give for not exercising are: no time, no equipment, no place, no money.

- The lack of time shouldn't stop you from improving your health and life expectancy. It is now well-documented that 30 minutes three times a week is all that is needed to create good health and even moderate amounts of exercise can help protect against early death.
- Exercise will maintain strong muscles, allowing an active and independent lifestyle. It increases endurance and vitality.
- Expensive equipment is not necessary. A good pair of walking shoes and some comfortable clothes will do.
- It isn't necessary to join an expensive health club. It costs nothing to take a walk – pick a location where it is both safe and convenient and get healthy.
- Motivation is a matter of 'skill power', not will-power. You are in charge of changing your behaviour.

Barrier	Solution
You don't know how it will benefit you.	Find out how it will affect your blood pressure, weight, cholesterol, flexibility and strength.
You fear over-exertion.	Get a baseline health evaluation.
You don't have time.	Set aside time on your calendar – a week at a time.
You procrastinate.	Place the proper clothes near your bed so you see them first thing in the morning.
You can't make a long-term commitment.	Plan a week at a time. Select differing activities, those you enjoy.
No will-power.	Exercise with a friend – this will help with motivation.
You don't see improvement.	Keep track of progress. Distance, weight, body measurements or length of exertion.

EYE BAGS

Everyone has awakened in the morning, looked into the mirror and found what appears to be several satchels underneath their eyes.

As you age, your skin loses some of its elasticity and muscles within your eyelids lose tone. Fat from your eye socket can migrate forward and accumulate in your eyelid. Also, fluids can accumulate and cause the familiar eye bags.

- Allergies as well as smoking can cause swelling and aggravate the problem.
- Cut down on fluids before bedtime.
- Reduce the salt in your diet as this tends to help in the retention of fluids.
- Get plenty of sleep.
- Apply a clean face cloth dipped in ice-water or a moist tea bag over your eyes for 15 minutes once or twice a day.

EYE DIFFICULTIES

Often the diagnostician uses an examination of the eyes to find clues to underlying ailments.

Some of the things that the doctor might be looking at and which you can use to zero in on your own ailments are:

- Watery eyes are common with the common cold.
- Protruding eyes are often a symptom of a thyroid problem.
- Dark circles under the eyes, as well as red, itchy and swollen eyelids, can be indications of allergies.
- Yellowing of the white of the eyes is often symptomatic of disease of the liver or gall-bladder.
- Blurring of vision can be symptomatic of high blood pressure or diabetes.
- Droopy eyelids can be an early sign of myasthenia gravis.
- Pupil size that varies between the eyes can be an indication of tumour.

Any of these signs of further disease require treatment by a doctor, unless it is quite clear that they are minor, such as the watery eyes with a cold.

- Bloodshot eyes can be treated with an eyewash made of camomile tea, allowed to cool.
- Blurred vision can be aided by adding vitamin A and potassium to the diet.
- Dry eyes can be helped with the addition of vitamin A to the diet.
- Itchy eyes can be aided by supplementing the diet with vitamin B complex.

- Photophobia can also be aided by adding vitamin A to the diet.
- Eyes that are stuck shut with mucus in the morning should be washed out separately with a solution of eyebright or a boric acid wash. Use a clean compress for each eye to avoid transferring any infectious material from one eye to the other.

The eyes require a great of deal of oxygen and other nutrients for health. They also need to be rested frequently to avoid eyestrain and pain behind the eye.

- Avoid close reading in improper light.
- Avoid smoke-filled rooms and environmental pollutants.
- If the eyes feel fatigued, lie down with cold compresses made with camomile tea on each eye.
- Do not use eyedrops to get rid of redness, as repeated use will result in a rebound condition, calling for more eyedrops the next time the eyes feel fatigued.
- Avoid nicotine, sugar and caffeine as they may sometimes have a temporary affect on the clarity of vision.

EYEBROW PLUCKING

You don't want to look like the Neanderthal with your brows growing in a straight line across the bridge of your nose, but you find it too painful to pluck them.

- Try numbing the area of the brow with an ice-cube just prior to plucking.
- Immediately place a cotton ball soaked in witch-hazel to the area to decrease redness and swelling which can result if many hairs are removed at once.

EYELASHES

All of us dream of a sweep of long luxuriant lashes over our cheeks when we look downwards. Unfortunately, genetics control just how thick and long the eyelashes are.

However, lashes can be abused by frequent harsh face washing or eye rubbing with the hands and a little gentle treatment will encourage them to grow to the best of their inherited ability.

- Eyelashes can be encouraged to grow longer, thicker and more rapidly by applying castor oil nightly to the tips of clean lashes.

FACIAL HAIR

We've all heard the old joke: 'Who won the Miss Greece contest?' Answer: 'The one without the moustache.'

Facial hair is a problem for many women as long as we live in a culture that declares it unfeminine.

- Shaving is not a good option for women, as it soon grows back with a stiff stubble.
- Try depilatory creams. They dissolve unwanted hair but can cause skin irritations. Try a patch test first.
- Bleaching is a good solution for small amounts of hair. It makes the hair less visible, but as the hair grows, it will come back in its original colour.
- Plucking is not a good option for hair on the upper lip but is good for eyebrow hair.
- Electrolysis is the only permanent solution to excessive facial hair: it destroys the hair root so it will not grow back.

FALLS

Falling is one of the most common causes for individuals over age 65 to lose their independence.

Before a fall sidelines you, take a fall-prevention inventory.

- Have your vision and hearing checked regularly, so you don't lose important cues that help you maintain your balance.
- Exercise regularly: it improves strength, muscle tone and coordination.
- Ask about the medications you take – some may affect balance and coordination.
- Avoid alcohol – even a little alcohol can affect balance and reflexes.
- Get up slowly – you can become dizzy if you stand up too quickly.
- Maintain balance and footing – wear sturdy, low-heeled shoes with wide, non-slip soles.
- In your home, remove raised doorway thresholds, fasten area carpets, don't use throw rugs.
- Be sure stairways are well-lighted and have a sturdy hand rail.
- Install grab handles and non-skid mats inside baths.
- Don't use hard-to-reach shelves in kitchens.
- Never stand on a chair.

- Use non-skid floor wax and wipe spills immediately.
- Use a night light in the bedroom, so as to avoid walking around furniture in the dark.

FAT MEASUREMENT

Are you really overweight?

Your scales won't tell you and neither will your clothing. What you really need to know is how much of your total body weight is made up of fat.

You may look slim, you may have lost weight, but you might really be over-fat. The ideal is no more than 16 per cent for men and 20 per cent for women.

- Pinch a fold of skin from the upper side of your upper arm, midway up the back of your thigh, and at one side of your abdomen, just below your waist.
- Measure the thickness of this pinch of flesh with a ruler or a caliper. If you can pinch less than 1 inch, your body fat level is OK. Every $1/4$ inch above that represents 10 pounds of excess fat.

FATIGUE

Are you struggling to get started in the morning? Is your first thought when that alarm clock goes off, "Oh, no, not already!"? Do you yearn for a nap after lunch and fall into an easy chair when you get home at night?

Getting more energy is a matter of thinking about what you can do about it, unless there is some medical reason for your fatigue – it's a matter of attitude.

- Begin with eating a good breakfast, not just a doughnut and coffee – that only gives you the sugar blues to start your day.
- Set specific goals for each day. If you want to begin exercising, make a plan about how you are going to do that and when. Working out gives you energy – you will feel better after you exercise.
- If you think you have too much to do and you just get tired thinking about it all, break it into manageable portions. The old, 'one thing at a time' adage will make tasks easier. And learn to delegate tasks. You don't have to do everything yourself.
- Give up smoking, it robs you of oxygen. Breathe.
- Alcohol is a depressant: that drink before dinner may be part of the problem.

- Before you fall into that easy chair in the evening, plan what you will do with your time if you DON'T turn on the television.
- Take a holiday. Recharge your emotional batteries.
- If you are feeling a lot of anger or hostility, deal with the problem and then redirect that energy.
- If you still feel fatigued, while it might mean that you need to manage your life better, it could also be a signal of a more serious illness, so see your doctor.

FEVER

Fever is not an illness – it is a symptom of one. It is the body's defence mechanism in operation against infection.

Fever is a normal function of the body's immune system. It tells you that the body is busy waging war on foreign invaders, such as the bacteria that causes an infection. Sometimes the temperature is localised, as when the skin surrounding a cut feels warm to the touch, indicating that the body's disease fighting system is fighting microbes at that location.

- If a fever does not go above 102 degrees F in adults or 103 degrees F in children, it is best to allow it to run its course. The immune system is at work – fighting the invading microbes.
- Never give children aspirin, as it has been implicated in Reye's syndrome, a serious disease.
- Drink plenty of fluids and juices. It is best to avoid solid foods until the body temperature has returned to normal.
- Cool sponge baths will aid in reducing the fever.
- Avoid chilling the body while drying off.
- You might want to try inserting sliced onions or peeled garlic cloves into some socks and wearing them along the bottoms of your feet. This will soon bring the fever down.
- Make a tea with $1/2$ teaspoonful of cayenne pepper in boiling water, add some honey and orange juice and drink throughout the day.
- Take the usual precautions to avoid contact with individuals with colds and other contagious illnesses.
- Wash hands thoroughly and regularly during the day and keep your hands off of your face. Bacteria and viruses transferred from your hands to your nasal area can quickly cause an infection such as a cold or flu.
- Clean any cuts, scrapes or abrasions, as an intact skin is your first line

of defence against microbes which enter the body through these types of injuries.

FIBROCYSTIC DISEASE OF THE BREAST

You slide your soapy hand over your breast in the shower and suddenly you feel a lump. Your first thought is, "Is it cancer?"

You need a thorough examination by your doctor to be sure, but often it is fibrocystic disease.

When these round lumps move freely within the breast when pressed they probably are benign. Such lumps feel similar to the eyeball felt by the fingertips against the eyelid. They may be painful or tender prior to menstruation and often change in size. These lumps become fluid-filled, forming a cyst, and then fibrous tissue surrounds the cyst and thickens like a scar. It is the pressure of this fibrous tissue that causes the pain.

- Change your diet to one that is low in fat and high in fibre. This type of diet will aid you in metabolising oestrogen differently.
- Keep your weight down because fat acts like an extra gland, producing and storing more oestrogen than is good for you.
- Avoid diuretics as they deplete potassium and contribute to the problem of lumpy breasts.
- Take primrose oil or borage oil for essential fatty acids which help mobilise the fluid in the cysts so that the lymph glands can transport it properly.
- Avoid alcohol, animal fats, fried foods, salt, tobacco and sugar.
- Avoid coffee, tea, cola drinks and chocolate. All of these items contain caffeine which has been highly implicated in the formation of these cysts.
- Wear a good support bra.
- Gentle massage with soapy hands during your daily shower will ease those breast fluids back into the lymph system.
- Perform a regular monthly self-breast examination, become aware of what breast cysts feel like and after age 35 have a regular mammogram.

FISSURES

It hurts to smile because of those tiny cracks at the corners of your mouth and it definitely hurts when you move your bowels.

A fissure is a break or tear in the skin. Both the oral and anal variety can occur where skin meets delicate mucous membrane.

Anal fissures are usually caused by the passage of hard stools and the cause is usually a diet lacking in fibre.

- Lubricate the anal canal with petroleum jelly before each bowel movement.
- Eat more fruit, vegetables and whole grains and drink six to eight glasses of water each day.
- After a shower or bowel movement, dust your anal area with baby powder to keep this area dry while it heals.
- Avoid hot spicy foods.
- Wipe or pat gently after a bowel movement, do not use coloured toilet paper as it can be irritating to delicate tissue. Carry some pads moistened with witch-hazel with you in a plastic bag to use when away from home.
- Take a hot sitz bath to relax the anal sphincter and speed healing.
- Non-prescription topical creams containing hydrocortisone can be very helpful in reducing inflammation.

Oral fissures usually occur in cold weather, when the lips become dry or chapped.

- Keep the lips well-lubricated, coating the tiny cracks with petroleum jelly to keep them moist until they heal.

FLATULENCE

So many jokes but not very funny if your stomach feels like the Goodyear blimp ... and your friends avoid getting in the lift with you.

Some people are gas producers and have a problem with flatulence a good part of the time.

- Many people who are lactose intolerant find that their flatulence is created by dairy products.
- Most of us are aware that beans are gas producers, but so are cabbage, broccoli, Brussels sprouts, onions, cauliflower, radishes, bananas, to name a few. Take a good look at your diet and go easy on the foods that create the problem for you.
- If you have been adding fibre to your diet for health reasons, it is best to add it slowly until your intestines become accustomed to it.
- Activated charcoal tablets, available at most chemists, will absorb much of the gas.
- Over-the-counter dimethicone has a defoaming action which prevents the

formation of mucous-surrounded gas pockets.

- Try some anise seeds, caraway seeds or dill seeds. Crush them and add to a cupful of boiling water. Steep and drink.
- A cupful of ginger tea after a gassy meal is useful. Make by adding $1/4$ teaspoonful of powdered ginger to a cupful of hot water. Drink slowly.
- Lie on the floor and bring your knees up to your chest and down again. Repeat until you feel relief.

FOOD POISONING

It is time for the family picnic or the soccer game in the heat of the summer. A blanket spread out on the beach with lots of food, waiting for everyone to come out of the water, just sitting there in the sun. The perfect place for microbes to grow.

Food poisoning occurs when a person eats food that contains harmful bacteria. The most common cause of this is *Salmonella bacteria* which are part of the natural intestinal make-up of animals. This bacteria is easily transmitted through knives, table tops, contact with other food products and the hands of those who prepare the food.

In addition, raw or poorly cooked animal products are another source of damaging bacteria. When meat is ground up it is difficult to remove the intestinal contents and it is most important that this type of meat be very thoroughly cooked.

Symptoms of food poisoning include nausea, vomiting, mild abdominal pain, diarrhoea and dehydration. Often diarrhoea is the first sign of food poisoning. This initial diarrhoea is the body's first line of defence in ridding itself of the toxic bacteria as rapidly as possible.

The next most common source of food poisoning is *Staphylococcus aureus*, a micro-organism found in the nose and throat of humans. A frequent source of this contamination is food which is laid out at a salad bar or buffet table and is accessible to the sneezes, coughs and unwashed hands of many people.

- Food kept at room temperature encourages the growth of bacteria. The 'keep it hot or keep it cold' rule is an excellent one to follow to avoid such illnesses.
- If you find yourself ill, fill up on fluids to replace those lost with the diarrhoea.
- Don't take products to stop the diarrhoea; this is Nature's method of flushing out the toxins.

- Don't attempt to induce vomiting, it isn't necessary.
- Within a few hours after the diarrhoea and vomiting have subsided, you will be ready for food, but go easy – your stomach is still feeling a little tender. Start with bland foods, like cereal, crackers or a little clear broth.
- After a day or two, you will begin to feel like eating a few of the things you regularly like and then you will know you are on the way to recovery.
- Keep all perishables refrigerated.
- Cook all animal products and fish thoroughly.
- Wash your hands thoroughly before handling food.
- Clean all utensils which come in contact with raw meats.
- Dispose of any foods which have grown mould, such as bacon, luncheon meats, hot dogs, peanut butter.
- Thaw all frozen foods in the refrigerator, not on the table top.

FOOD SAFETY ON OUTINGS

Nobody wants to be sick at a picnic – so be wise, take precautions in the preparation of foods to make sure everyone has a good and safe time.

- Use an insulated cooler. Put ice on top with goods at the bottom, as the cold travels downwards.
- Pack things straight from the refrigerator. Don't line things up on the table for a period of time before packing the cooler. Things should be cold to the touch before going into the cooler.
- Wrap all foods separately. Don't place food directly on ice that is not of drinking water quality. Keep raw meat, poultry or fish well wrapped.
- Don't put the cooler in the hot car-boot. Keep the car in the shade at the picnic. And keep the lid on the cooler at all times.
- Keep food and utensils covered until serving time. Flies, other insects and household pets can carry the *Salmonella bacteria* responsible for food poisoning.
- Keep hot foods hot. Use a vacuum flask or insulated dish for serving.
- Clean your hands. Take along disposable hand cleaning wipes to use before and after working with food.
- Remember the two-hour rule. Return leftovers to the cooler as quickly as possible. Two hours is the maximum time food should be left unrefrigerated. If the ice has melted, discard perishable leftovers.

FOOT WOES

We mistreat them terribly. We squash them into shoes that are too small, we totter around on high heels, we make them carry us through shopping centres for endless hours. No wonder they bark at us.

After a long hard day of trotting around all over town, your feet deserve a little pampering:

- Elevate them. Sit down, put your feet up and wiggle your toes to get the circulation moving.
- Soak those weary feet in a warm bath with 2 tablespoonfuls of Epsom salts. Pat dry and massage in some nice lotion or hand cream.
- Massage your feet with baby oil. Rub the oil over the entire foot, squeezing the toes gently and then pressing in a circular motion over the bottoms.
- Or, wrap a few ice-cubes in a flannel and rub over your feet for a few minutes for a really refreshing stimulation.
- Change heel heights. If you wear high heels all day, you are going to suffer from tightened calf muscles.
- Add an insole to your shoe to give additional padding under the ball of your foot.

FRECKLES

Freckles are sprinkled across your nose and you notice that you have more of them in the summer. You dream of having freckleless skin. Is it possible?

Freckles are brownish pigmented spots on the skin and they are mostly hereditary.

- Avoid sunlight, use a sunscreen to keep them at a minimum.
- Eliminate sugar from your diet; it is implicated in their excessive production.
- Try a concealer.
- Apply a bleaching cream or lemon juice at bedtime, as this will lighten them.
- Many people find freckles attractive, so learn to love yours.

FRIGIDITY

You have little or no interest in sex. You are too tired, too busy, too stressed out, too worried. The "not tonight dear", might just be coming from either or both of the sexual partners.

If you want to make some changes, try some of the following suggestions from Masters and Johnson:

- Make an appointment to spend 15 minutes together each day.
- Make a date. Take a walk together in the evening, find some activity you both enjoy, and share it.
- Schedule a weekend away together.
- Go to bed at the same time.
- Relax together, take a shower together or give each other a massage.
- Take the television out of the bedroom. When you go to bed, go there either to sleep or to make love.
- Try hugging and kissing without the expectation of sex being the result.
- Forget alcohol and drugs; they dampen sexual abilities.

FROSTBITE

You can get lost, find yourself stranded in the middle of winter on an unfamiliar road, or go hunting and suddenly find you were not prepared for a sudden drop in temperature. The risk and extent of cold injury is increased by heat loss (wet clothing, contact with metal, wind chill).

When the body needs to conserve heat, blood flow is shifted away from the skin, where much heat would be lost through radiation. This lack of blood causes pain and if the blood flow is significantly reduced for a long enough period of time, gangrene may result from this prolonged poor circulation.

- Find shelter from the wind; wind chill can be a significant factor in frostbite.
- Don't use a heat-lamp or a camp-fire to rewarm. Frostbitten skin is easily burned.
- Don't rub with snow, as this just causes friction.
- Wear mittens: they are warmer than gloves.
- Keep your head covered. Heat loss from the head accounts for a major portion of the easily lost body heat.
- Drinking alcohol actually causes you to lose more heat.

- Keep moving.
- If you are stranded, stay with your vehicle.
- Rewarm any frostbitten parts with warm water as soon as possible.

FUNGUS INFECTIONS

These infections burn, seem to appear suddenly and you wonder where they come from. Fungi and bacteria are a natural part of the environment and they thrive in any dark, damp atmosphere.

A fungus can infect almost any part of the body, particularly the skin, the vagina, between the toes or underneath the nails.

A depressed immune system can often allow a fungus to take hold which would not ordinarily infect a healthy individual. Individuals with HIV infections, those already ill from other disease, such as diabetes or other debilitating disease, are more likely to suffer from fungal infections.

Such infections are often evident by moist red patches on the body and if the infection is vaginal, a cheesy discharge will be present.

- Keep all body parts clean and dry, paying particular attention to areas where fungi can take hold, such as between the toes or underneath the nails for those who are wearing artificial nails.
- Anyone with a vaginal infection should wear underwear with a cotton gusset and avoid tight fitting clothing, such as stretch pants and jeans.
- For infected nails, soak the nails daily in a solution of warm water with a few drops of liquid bleach added and dry thoroughly.
- If wearing artificial nails, they should be removed immediately.
- To treat fungus on the skin, apply honey to the area and alternate with crushed garlic cloves. Repeat daily until the area of skin returns to normal.
- Avoid dairy products, which tend to increase mucus and provide a more fertile home for fungal growth.
- Take acidophilis tablets to provide friendly bacteria which combat the fungi.
- Take 3 to 5 garlic capsules daily to neutralise the fungi.

GALL-BLADDER DISEASE

The old saying, 'Fair, fat, female and forty' was thought to be true about who would suffer from gall-bladder disease – but it simply isn't true and anyone can have such a problem.

The gall-bladder's function is to hold the bile and concentrate it so that the body can use it to digest fats. The bile contains cholesterol, salts, lecithin and some other substances.

When the gall-bladder becomes inflamed, there is severe pain in the upper right abdomen and fever, nausea and vomiting. When the cholesterol in the gall-bladder crystallises and combines with the bile salts, gallstones are formed. When a stone blocks the duct from the gall-bladder there is severe pain, nausea and vomiting. This often follows the eating of fatty foods.

- A fast, with only water taken, will reduce the inflammation of the organ itself. When the pain has subsided, the fast should be broken with fruit juices, pear and apple juice, followed by the slow introduction of low-fat solid raw foods.
- If there are gallstones, take the juice of a lemon with four tablespoons of olive oil twice a day.
- Maintain your correct weight, as obesity is linked to gall-bladder disease.
- Fruit and vegetable juices are very beneficial.
- Avoid sugar and products which contain a large amount of fat and sugar such as biscuits and cakes. Avoid animal fat, fried foods, spicy foods, soft drinks, coffee and chocolate.
- Take some alfalfa tablets as they are rich in minerals.
- Take 3 tablespoonfuls of fresh lemon juice in a glass of warm water half an hour before breakfast. Lemon juice is said to cleanse and stimulate the gall-bladder to work.

GLAUCOMA

If you experience some sudden eye pain, blurred vision or see a halo around lights, or lose your peripheral vision, it could be glaucoma.

Glaucoma is a progressive eye disease which is a leading cause of blindness. The cause is unknown, but stress, heredity and nutritional imbalances are implicated. There are medications and surgical treatments for the various types of glaucoma, and any of the symptoms require medical attention.

- Take 100 mg of vitamin B2, along with B-complex daily, as an imbalance of B vitamins has been implicated in glaucoma.
- Take 500 mg buffered vitamin C with rutin to reduce pressure behind the eye.
- Avoid alcohol and all products containing caffeine as they tend to elevate the pressure inside the eye.
- Avoid smokers as they pollute the atmosphere which is particularly

irritating to any eye which lacks moisture.
- Bathe the eyes with warm eye baths with herbs such as camomile or fennel as they are beneficial and soothing.

GOUT

The pain can strike in the middle of the night like a red hot poker and you don't have to be King Henry VIII to suffer from it. Gout is a recurring acute arthritis of joints which results from the deposition in and about the joints and tendons of crystals of monosodium urate.

Gout may become chronic and deforming. The majority of sufferers of gout are men.

Various underlying abnormalities of purine metabolism, both genetic and acquired, may be responsible for the problem. An attack usually appears without warning, but may be precipitated by minor trauma (as from poorly fitting shoes), overindulgence in food or alcohol, fatigue, infections or treatment with diuretics. The first attack may come without warning, at night. The pain becomes progressively more severe and is often described as throbbing, crushing or excruciating. There are usually signs of an acute inflammatory response with swelling, warmth, redness and tenderness. The skin is tense, hot, shiny, and dusky red or purplish in colour.

The joint of the big toe is involved most frequently, but the instep, ankle, knee, wrist and elbow are also common sites. In early attacks, only a single joint may be affected but in later attacks, two or more joints can be affected simultaneously. Systemic reactions may include fever, tachycardia, chills and malaise. The first few attacks usually last only a few days, but later untreated attacks may persist for several weeks.

Uric acid is a by-product of certain foods, those that are purine-rich.
- Keep the affected joint elevated and rest.
- Take an over-the-counter anti-inflammatory medication such as ibuprofen and follow the bottle directions. Aspirin can make gout worse by inhibiting excretion of uric acid.
- Apply ice for about 10 minutes at a time.
- Be sure to have an abundant fluid intake to combat dehydration and flush the uric acid out of the system.
- The urine should be alkalinised with sodium bicarbonate.
- Eat no red meat as this contains extremely high amounts of uric acid.
- Avoid purine-rich foods such as anchovies, asparagus, herrings, meat

gravies, mushrooms, mussels, all organ meats, sardines and sweetbreads.
- The closer you stay to a vegetarian diet, the less gout will trouble you.
- Alcohol increases the production of uric acid and must be eliminated from the diet entirely.
- A weight reduction programme should be carefully monitored and rapid weight loss should be avoided as this could result in increased uric acid levels, which would then precipitate an additional bout of the illness.
- Increase your intake of cherries and cherry juice which have been shown to neutralise uric acid.
- Soak the suffering joint in a bath made from warm comfrey tea.

GREASY HAIR

Your hair is as flat as a pancake. You want bounce, volume, curls. The oil from your scalp glands wicks onto fine straight hair quickly. No matter how much you shampoo and curl, your hair is lank and separated into greasy strands by the end of the day. People with fine hair have more hairs per inch of scalp, and with more hair goes more oil glands. Heat and humidity encourage your oil glands to get to work and so can changes in your hormones.
- Shampoo frequently, once a day if necessary.
- A clear see-through shampoo is best, as it contains fewer conditioners.
- Do not use a conditioner, it only adds layers of stuff to coat your hair. If you think you must use a conditioner, add it only to the tips of your hair.
- Use an astringent of witch-hazel on your scalp. Apply it with cotton-wool balls to the scalp only, not the hair.
- Brushing brings the oil from the scalp down the length of the hair. Brush only enough to detangle.
- Select your hair-stylist carefully. Tell them that you want a 'body' cut. Don't wear your hair long and one length; layers will give the illusion of more volume.
- Relax. When you are under stress you produce more androgen which will stimulate your oil glands to overwork.
- Excessively greasy hair can be caused by the birth control pill.
- Rinse with a mixture of lemon juice and water, as this will cut through the grease.
- Rinse with apple cider vinegar to remove any soap residue.
- Styling gels and mousse clog the pores of the scalp, so try to style without them.

GRIEF

Grief can follow any loss; a loved one, a job, a divorce, a long illness.

Some people take longer than others to get over their loss. Don't rush it and don't ignore it.

- Don't hide your emotions, let them out.
- Get support from family members or friends.
- Vent your emotions in a constructive manner: write out your feelings in a diary or pursue some very physical outlet for your feelings.
- Avoid alcohol, as it only dampens the pain for a short time.
- Don't spend special days alone; share them with someone else.
- Put off any major decisions or life changes until your thinking is clearer.
- Eat well and get sufficient rest.
- Expect some temporary setbacks: just when you think you are better, grief can come back. Continue to work through your loss.

GUM DISEASE

The dentist says, "Your teeth are fine, no cavities." But before you can breathe that sigh of relief, he adds, "But your gums are swollen and bleeding."

Gum (*periodontal*) disease affects the tissue and bone that surrounds and supports your teeth. This includes gums, the bony tooth sockets and the connective tissue that secures each tooth to bone.

Gum disease is caused by plaque, a sticky, colourless film of bacteria that coats your teeth. If allowed to harden (calcify) the film turns into tartar.

When this tartar builds up, it can irritate your gums and create pockets of bacteria between your gums and teeth. This accumulation of bacteria, and your body's reaction to it, can destroy the tissue and bone supporting your teeth.

Gingivitis – Plaque and tartar buildup along the gum line. This can make gums dusky red, swollen, tender and prone to bleeding.

Periodontitis – This is the advanced stage of gum disease. If plaque and tartar extend beneath your gum line, destructive bacteria can multiply in this dark, airless region.

- Take the time to brush and floss properly. That old lick-and-a-promise just won't do.
- Brush thoroughly at the gum line.
- Alternate between two toothbrushes, allowing one to dry thoroughly before re-using.

- Increase the amount of calcium in your diet to increase your underlying bone.
- Stop smoking: smoking slows your gums' ability to heal themselves.
- Pick the right toothbrush: one with soft, rounded or polished bristles makes it possible to insert the brush at the gum line.
- Buy fluoride toothpaste, as this will help remove plaque while protecting against cavities.
- Brush twice daily, just before bedtime and again in the morning. During sleep, saliva flow lessens.
- Flossing removes plaque between your teeth and helps massage your gums.
- Increase your vitamin C to at least 500 mg daily to strengthen the gum tissue.
- Rinse with hydrogen peroxide mixed with water several times a week to inhibit bacteria growth.
- Eat raw vegetables as they will stimulate the teeth and gums.
- Occasionally brush with aloe vera gel to aid in healing bleeding gums.

HAEMORRHOIDS

Haemorrhoids are both painful and embarrassing – but 8 out of 10 people will have them sometimes during their lifetime – so if you find having them embarrassing – you have lots of company.

Haemorrhoids are swollen veins around the anus. They are usually caused by constipation, improper diet, lack of exercise, a chronic cough, prolonged periods of sitting, heavy lifting, obesity and sometimes liver damage. The symptoms are itching and bleeding, with discomfort and pain.

Small haemorrhoids which are uncomplicated or cause only slight bleeding at infrequent intervals do not require any treatment beyond efforts to correct the underlying cause.

- Adding bulk to your diet by increasing the raw fruits and vegetables can keep your bowel movements soft.
- A stool softener (psyllium) in a glass of water several times a day and followed by an additional glass of water may prevent the pain and straining caused by passage of large, hard stools.
- Avoid trauma to the tender area when cleansing after bowel movements by patting rather than rubbing the area with a soft tissue slightly dampened with witch-hazel.

- A warm sitz bath can relieve the pain.
- Apply a poultice made from elderberry herbs to relieve pain.
- Be sure to drink plenty of fluids daily.

The people of those cultures where unrefined foods are not a staple of the diet rarely suffer from haemorrhoids. Apples, beets, broccoli, carrots, green beans, oat bran, peas, pears and whole grains should be included in the diet.

- Forget medicated suppositories. They go too far into the rectum to do any good. Instead, lubricate one finger covered by a finger sheath with haemorrhoid cream and apply to the interior edge of the anus as well as the outside several times a day and after a bowel movement.
- Avoid reading on the toilet, as this can contribute to the difficulty by encouraging the reader to sit too long. Prolonged sitting encourages engorgement of these veins.
- Regular exercise strengthens the abdominal muscles and aids in the mobilisation of the food through the intestines.
- Avoid heavy lifting.
- Use witch-hazel directly on external haemorrhoids for pain relief – it causes the blood vessels to contract.
- Coffee, spices, beer and cola drinks are thought to contribute to the problem, so avoid them until you feel better.
- Try applying one of the over-the-counter cortisone creams directly to the tissue to help in healing.

HAIR

It is so easy to abuse your hair. Perms, colouring, bleaches, electric curlers, daily blow-drying, exposure to the elements. So then, what do you do when your hair looks like the kitchen mop?

- Use a conditioner; it will bring the cuticle of the hair shaft back against the shaft.
- Protect your hair from the elements by wearing a hat.
- Wear a bathing-cap when swimming; chlorine in pools is extremely damaging.
- Try mashing very ripe bananas together with an avocado, apply to your hair for about 15 minutes and rinse.
- If you suffer from oily hair, shampoo frequently with a shampoo recommended for a baby's hair and forget the conditioner: you don't need more goo.

- Don't over-brush your hair, this just carries the oil from the scalp throughout your hair.
- Rinse with the juice of a couple of lemons in warm water; they will aid in reducing the oil and give your hair a great shine.
- Frizzy hair can be tamed with an apple cider vinegar rinse made with a couple of tablespoonfuls in warm water plus one tablespoonful of wheat germ oil. This will also act as a tonic for the scalp.
- Thin hair can be given more volume by adding 2 egg whites and the juice of a lemon to your shampoo.
- There is no known remedy for hair loss but the drug Minoxidil has been shown to slow or retard hair loss. It is normal to lose 50 to 100 hairs daily.

HOLIDAYS

Don't let the holiday of your dreams turn into a nightmare. Do some advance planning.

- Be sure your immunisations are up to date.
- Take along all your usual medications.
- Don't pack your medications in a bag that goes in the luggage compartment. Take it with you in your hand luggage.
- Keep all medications in their original containers to avoid any difficulties with Customs.
- Keep all medications out of the heat and humidity.
- Take a traveller's first aid kit.
- Allow yourself plenty of time to get to your destination so you don't arrive all stressed out.
- Don't overeat, try to avoid having too many different and exotic foods.
- Get sufficient rest and sleep.
- Schedule your return so you will have a day to recover before you have to go back to work.

HANDWASHING

You find yourself complaining, "I've had three or four colds already this year – I really need a holiday."

The simplest way to avoid such repeated infections is to WASH YOUR HANDS.

- When the cold and flu season is underway, the most important thing you can do to protect yourself from the sneezes and sniffles of others is to wash your hands – at least three times a day.
- Between handwashings, try to keep your hands away from your nose and eyes. Thorough handwashing isn't simple. You need to apply soap to your hands and rub vigorously for at least 10 seconds to suspend the germs and then rinse them away. Water warm enough to cut through grease is best (110 degrees Fahrenheit). Germs tend to accumulate around the cuticles, beneath the fingernails and in the creases of the hands, so concentrate on these areas.
- Always wash:
  - ☐ Before you handle or eat food.
  - ☐ After using the bathroom.
  - ☐ After changing a nappy after handling uncooked food (especially meat).
  - ☐ After handling money.
  - ☐ After blowing your nose, sneezing or coughing into your hand.
  - ☐ After playing with a pet.
  - ☐ After handling kitchen waste.

HANGNAILS

Hangnails are those annoying little splits of skin at the edges of your fingernails that seem to catch on everything you touch and amaze you how painful and inflamed they can be. They are frequent in those who have their hands in water a lot or bite their nails.

They are nothing more than little tags of dry skin, until they become inflamed or infected. If they become infected, they can lead to a serious inflammation of the cuticles.

- Moisten with oil first, then clip off with sterilised scissors.
- If the hangnail is really sore, apply some antibiotic cream and put a plaster over the finger until the redness is gone.
- If you work with a lot of paper (which tends to take the oil out of your hands) or you work with your hands in water frequently, remember to moisturise your hands and particularly your cuticles daily.

HANGOVER

You wake up with an entire corps of flamenco dancers stomping on your skull. Unfortunately, the only thing that will really help you feel better is time, but there are a few things you can do to help get you through the day and relieve some of the symptoms – such as headache and nausea.

- Before your fall into bed the night before the morning after, drink one glass of fruit juice and swallow one 500 mg vitamin C tablet, plus one glass of water for each drink you had (if possible). You'll thank yourself in the morning.
- Drink fruit juice or tomato juice – either one will accelerate the removal of the alcohol from your system.
- Eat some crackers and honey in the morning. They will aid in avoiding nausea and the honey will provide you with a concentrated source of fructose, the sugar that aids in metabolising the alcohol.
- Take something over-the-counter for your headache, but only after you have something in your stomach.
- Drink some broth which will help replace the salt and potassium you lose through the action of alcohol (a diuretic).
- Drink lots of water.
- When you feel a little better, take a vitamin B complex capsule, as alcohol drains these vitamins from your body.
- Drink some coffee to constrict the blood vessels in your head which are contributing to the pounding headache you have.
- Be sure to get a good night's sleep the following night – you should feel better in 24 hours.
- It is best to try to avoid that hangover in the first place.
- Try not to be a hearty-party animal. You really don't need to be the life of the party. Slow it down, no more than an ounce of alcohol an hour.
- Eat a good meal before you start to drink: it will definitely lessen the hangover.
- Avoid drinks that contain substances known as congeners. These are other kinds of alcohols found in most alcoholic beverages – vodka has the least – champagne and cognac the most.

HAY FEVER

You sneeze, your nose runs, your eyes are watery and you feel all-over miserable but while you know it's not a cold – it seems to last forever.

Hay fever is a reaction which affects the mucous membranes of the nose, eyes and breathing passages. It can be caused by any variety of inhalants. Dust, pollen (from growing things such as grass, trees and flowers), feathers and animal dander are the most frequent culprits.

Individual reactions will often vary because there are differing pollens throughout the year.

Spring type is usually due to tree pollens, summer type to grass and weed pollens, autumn type due to weed pollens and occasionally, it can be due primarily to airborne fungus spores.

- If possible, the allergen should avoided. Your home should be made as dust free as possible. Curtains and carpeting should be either cleaned frequently or removed entirely, if they are the cause.
- Pets should be bathed frequently and the sufferer should avoid petting the animals. If you touch the animals, wash your hands before touching your face.
- Add an air filter to your home air-conditioning system.
- If a home humidifier is used, it should be cleaned thoroughly as it is frequently the source of fungus spores.
- If you know what substance creates your hay fever, it makes sense to do your best to avoid the allergen.
- Take 1,500 mg buffered vitamin C. Include some bioflavonoids from the rind of orange or lemon, sweetened with honey. The need for vitamin C seems to be greater in those with allergies. Eat a daily grapefruit or orange.
- Vitamin-rich watercress is known to be a powerful anti-allergen. Add it to salads and sandwiches.

HEADACHE

"Not tonight, my dear, I have a headache."

All the movies in the world have made a joke of that killer of the love scene. Maybe you haven't excused yourself from the romance department with that line, but there is hardly a person alive who hasn't had a headache at one time or another.

During a headache, the level of serotonin, a brain chemical, drops. A message is then sent to the blood vessels in the brain's outer covering. These blood vessels relax, become inflamed and swell. Your brain then receives the pain message and the result is: a headache. Sometimes sinus pain, allergy and TMJ (temporomandibular joint syndrome) can be confused with a headache.

Something as simple as squinting in the bright sun can give you a headache. Besides eyestrain, hunger, too much alcohol, fever, too much or too little sleep, or exertion can cause what is termed a 'normal' headache. This type of head pain typically goes away by itself soon after what was causing it stops.

Nine out of ten headaches are caused by *tension*.

Migraine causes about six per cent of headaches and less then one per cent are *cluster headaches*. This type of headache seems to be linked to seasonal changes. Men, especially heavy smokers and heavy drinkers, get more cluster headaches than other people.

If the headache is accompanied by: blurred vision, sensitivity to light, food allergies, facial sinus pain, heart pounding, visual disturbances in colour and the feeling that your head is about to explode, consult a doctor, this may signal a more serious problem.

- For tension headaches, try heat or ice-packs, a hot shower or rest. Take a break from the stressful situation.
- For migraine: sleep; a nap in a dark, quiet room; pressing an ice-pack to the back of the neck.
- For cluster headaches: no alcohol.
- Keep a headache calendar for at least two months. This can often help you discover your headache 'triggers'. The most common triggers are:
  - ☐ Stress.
  - ☐ Diet.
  - ☐ Alcohol.
  - ☐ Tyramine – a chemical in such foods as aged cheese, Chianti wine and pickled herring.
  - ☐ Chocolate.
  - ☐ Caffeine – or lack of the drug.
  - ☐ Food additives, such as sodium nitrite in hot dogs or monosodium glutamate in many processed foods.

Other common triggers are:
- Change in the season.
- Change in sleep patterns.
- Fluctuations in hormone levels. Sensory irritations.

- Polluted air or stuffy rooms.
- A minimal dose of aspirin, acetaminophen or ibuprofen can relieve your pain.

Over the long term, combat headaches by:

- Controlling triggers.
- Limiting use of painkillers.
- Stopping smoking.
- Managing stress.
- Deep breathing – a great tension reliever.
- Wearing a headband – this will decrease blood flow to the scalp.
- Avoiding excessive noise.

HEALTHY EATING

You think you eat a healthy diet until you go over what you ate in the last 24 hours and then, whoops! Maybe you ought to start thinking about what those greasy French fries and cola drinks are doing to you.

The recommendation to eat five servings of fruit and vegetables daily is based on the fact that they can help you control your weight and reduce your risk of coronary heart disease and cancer. They contain virtually no fat and most have fibre. They are rich in a variety of vitamins, minerals and other chemicals that scientists believe may be related to disease prevention, particularly cancer protection.

One serving equals half a cupful of cooked vegetables, canned fruit or juice. Count one cupful of chopped vegetables or fruit, or a medium whole fruit, as one serving.

Here is how they may help protect your health:

- **Beta carotene** – Deep-yellow and dark-green vegetables are rich sources of beta carotene – a substance your body uses to make vitamin A.
  Sources: carrots, spinach, tomatoes, winter squash, sweet potatoes, pumpkin, papaya, cantaloup, apricots and water melon.
- **Vitamins C and E** – These act as antioxidants. They fight free radicals – molecules that may cause disease by injuring cells or harming your body's natural healing ability.
  Sources: broccoli, oranges, Brussels sprouts, grapefruit, strawberries, cantaloup, cauliflower and baked potatoes. Vegetable oils, nuts, leafy greens and whole grains contain vitamin E.
- **Phytochemicals** – These are contained naturally in fruits, vegetables and

grains. Substances in cruciferous vegetables may be related to cancer protection.

Sources: Brussels sprouts, cauliflower, broccoli, kale, mustard greens, cabbage, turnips, garlic, flax seed, parsley and celery.

- **Fibre** – It is recommended that you eat 20 to 30 grams of fibre daily. Fibre lowers your risk of colon and rectal cancer.

  Sources: Fruits and vegetables, especially legumes. Half a cupful of cooked vegetables provides an average of 5 grams of fibre and less than 1 gram of fat. Legumes include split peas, black-eyed peas and lentils, kidney, pinto, black, navy and garbanzo beans.

  Diets with five servings of fruits and vegetables contain about 17 grams of fibre. Adding just two slices of wholewheat bread brings the total to approximately 20 grams of fibre.

- **Low fat** – In diets with no fruits and vegetables, fat contributed about 38 per cent of daily calories. Eating two servings of vegetables and at least three servings of fruit lowered daily calories from fat to approximately 34 per cent.

- Limiting fat to no more than 20 per cent of daily calories, you may reduce your risk of obesity, coronary, heart disease and cancer.

Ideas to get those five daily servings

- Eat soup – Use vegetables and legumes as a base for soups.
- Moisturise lean meats – Add raw, grated vegetables (carrots, potatoes or apples) to make meat loaf or meatballs.
- Thicken sauces without fat – Substitute cooked and puréed vegetables for cream or whole milk.
- Be creative – Pasta and stir-fry dishes are ideal ways to serve lots of different vegetables and reduce the amount of meat.
- Enhance old standbys – Add fruit to your breakfast cereal and raw, grated vegetables or fruit to muffins and cakes.
- Try new and unusual vegetables – You may find that by adding untried vegetables to soup you create a taste for them.
- Don't let lettuce limit salads – Choose a wider variety of greens, including chicory, collards, dandelion greens, kale, mustard greens, spinach and watercress.

HEARING LOSS

Does everyone around you mumble? Does everyone ask you to turn down the radio or the television? These are signs of gradual, age-related hearing loss.

- Hold a watch to your ear. If you can't hear it, it is time to have your hearing checked by a professional.
- Hearing aids, along with some self-help, can make hearing improvements.
- Ask people to speak clearly and in a normal tone of voice, not shouting at you.
- Look at people when they speak: you can learn a lot from their facial expressions.
- Limit background noise when you can.
- Sit near the front in theatres.
- Pay attention: lots of the things you didn't hear correctly were because you weren't really listening.

HEARTBURN

Lunch on the run, eat in the car with tomato ketchup running down your arm, wash it all down with a carton of ice-cream and maybe a beer. What next? Heartburn is now just a few minutes away and you'll soon be saying, "I can't believe I ate all that." Heartburn results from a backup of acid-containing stomach contents into your oesophagus.

- You can avoid heartburn by thinking before you eat.
- Eat smaller meals. Too much food expands your stomach and puts pressure on the band of muscle that helps keep food in your stomach.
- Avoid alcohol, fatty foods, chocolate, spearmint and peppermint. These foods can relax your oesophageal sphincter and promote upward flow of stomach contents.
- Use an antacid. Take one after meals and before bedtime.
- Don't eat before sleeping. Wait two or three hours after eating before lying down. This allows enough time for increased stomach acid produced by your last meal to taper off.
- Wear loose clothing. A tight belt or waistband can cause heartburn.
- Stop smoking. Nicotine relaxes the oesophageal sphincter.
- Elevate the head of your bed. Raising the head of your bed four to six

inches helps keep stomach acid in your stomach.
- Lose weight. Slimming helps reduce the pressure your abdomen puts on your stomach when you are lying down.
- Limit caffeine: it will irritate your sore oesophagus.
- Avoid carbonated drinks: they are a good source of heartburn.
- Try some relaxation to reduce your tension levels.

HEAT EXHAUSTION

You played a round of golf and then a set of tennis and you forgot your hat. Suddenly, you have a headache and begin to feel dizzy. You've overdone it in the heat.
- Get out of the sun right away.
- Drink some water to replace all that you have lost in sweating.
- If you suffer from heat exhaustion frequently, you need to eat more fruits and vegetables: they have a natural water content.
- Drink one of the sports drinks to replace both potassium and sodium.
- Do not use salt tablets, because they really don't replace essential minerals lost through sweating.
- Avoid alcohol, as it increases the already existing dehydration.
- Avoid caffeine, because it speeds dehydration too.
- Don't smoke. Smoking constricts blood vessels, keeping heat in the body.
- Slow down. Recognise that the heat can cause problems.
- Wear a hat.
- Keep your shirt on. Once you start to sweat, the shirt will help keep you cool.
- Wear light colours, because they reflect the sun's rays better than dark ones.
- Wear loosely woven fabrics which let your skin breathe.

HEPATITIS

Hepatitis is an inflammation in the liver. Three major causes of hepatitis are Type A and B viruses, alcohol and drugs. Rarer types include infectious mononucleosis, cytomegalovirus, as well as some other specific viral infections. Type A is spread primarily through faecal-oral contact, through water-and-food-borne routes. Ingestion of contaminated raw shellfish can be responsible.

Type B is transmitted through the blood. Transfusion of contaminated blood or blood products is one usual source, although the sharing of needles by drug users is also responsible, as well as some forms of sexual activity. This disease affects approximately 85 per cent of the homosexual community.

Hepatitis varies from a minor flu-like illness to fatal liver failure. It begins suddenly with anorexia, malaise, nausea, vomiting and fever. This flu-like stage can be slight or severe. Infectious hepatitis is contagious two to three weeks before and one week after the appearance of jaundice.

Hepatitis is a serious medical condition and should be treated by a doctor.

- Avoid all fats, alcohol, sugar and highly processed foods.
- Hands and all clothing should be washed often and bathrooms should be decontaminated frequently.
- Do not eat any raw fish or shellfish.
- A hepatitis B vaccine should be taken by all homosexuals, drug users and all those who work in the dental or medical professions.

HERPES, GENITAL AND ORAL

Genital herpes is a very prevalent sexually-transmitted disease but since we have heard so much about AIDS, we seldom hear much about genital herpes anymore. After an initial illness which feels very much like the flu, you have burning sores on your genitals. Most initial attacks of the ailment are the worst; hopefully subsequent attacks will be less severe.

Herpes simplex (Type I) is a viral disease which can cause cold sores which erupt around the lips and nostrils. After infection with this virus, it remains in the body throughout life. It can be dormant for years, recurring at various times. Illness, stress and a variety of unknown physical factors may cause an eruption at any time. Because of the increase in oral sexual activity, it is possible to have the Type I or Type II on either part of the body.

After the initial contact, the sores appear two to seven days after exposure. Recurrent eruptions are common but after a period of time, the virus burns itself out, rarely appearing after age 50. For individuals who have never had a cold sore (Type I), it is probable that you have had an exposure at an early age and developed antibodies to the virus.

A mild tingling or burning in the vaginal area may be the first sign of genital herpes in women. Within a matter of a few hours, blisters develop around the rectum, clitoris, and cervix, and in the vagina. There is often a watery discharge from the urethra and pain upon urination.

In men blisters break out on the penis, groin and scrotum, often with a urethral discharge and painful urination. Sometimes there will be painful swelling of the urethra and foreskin.

Both men and women often have a low-grade fever with muscular aching. The male may also have tender swollen lymph nodes in the groin. After a few days, pus erupts from the blisters and forms large, painful ulcers. These ulcers will crust over and dry while healing, usually leaving no scarring.

- Acyclovir by prescription can reduce the outbreaks, if taken on a regular basis. However, once the drug is stopped, it is possible a more serious outbreak can occur, with fever, extreme flu-like symptoms, nausea and vomiting.
- Avoid citrus products while having an outbreak, as citrus can make the urine more acid, creating more pain upon urination.
- To ease the pain and swelling, ice-packs can be applied to the area for 20 minutes at a time. Warm Epsom salts or baking soda baths can also be soothing to the pain.
- After the bath, pat the area dry gently and keep the lesions dry.
- Vitamin E cream alternating with vitamin A applied directly to the lesions can be helpful in speeding the healing.
- L-lysine cream is useful for some individuals.
- Avoid alcohol, colas, white flour products, sugar, refined carbohydrates and caffeine.
- Wear cotton underwear and practise good hygiene, keeping the lesions dry, particularly after urination.
- During an outbreak, women should carry a squirt bottle of water with them, so that they may flush the area with water after urination.
- Do not eat almonds, cashews, cereals, chicken, chocolate, dairy products, seeds, oatmeal or peanuts. These foods contain L-arginine, an amino acid that suppresses L-lysine, the amino acid that is thought to retard the growth of the virus.
- Avoid sexual intercourse with any individual who has active herpes lesions. It is best to use a condom to avoid transmission of the disease.
- Echinacea, myrrh and red clover capsules will aid in keeping the immune system in good condition. Goldenseal tea can be taken several times a day for the same reason.
- Six to ten garlic capsules a day will stimulate the immune system and aid in keeping this virus at bay.
- Zinc ointment is said to beneficial. Try it, it may work for you.
- If you have lesions you are contagious – avoid kissing or having sex.

HIATUS HERNIA

Nothing seems to stop your heartburn and belching and the doctor says you have a hiatus hernia. This may be the cause of your heartburn and belching, sometimes with an acid return up into the throat which causes a burning sensation. Occasionally there is a feeling of discomfort behind the breastbone.

A hiatus hernia is a protrusion of the stomach above the diaphragm through an opening in the muscles of the diaphragm. More than 40 per cent of the population over 40 years of age have a hiatus hernia, most of which are asymptomatic.

The cause is unknown. It is possibly genetic and is thought to be secondary to trauma. In populations where there is a high-fibre diet, hiatus hernia is less common as those individuals do not have to strain with bowel movements, thought to be one cause of the condition as straining puts pressure on the muscles of the diaphragm.

There is no specific treatment but any constant accompanying gastro-oesophageal reflux should be treated.

- Eat small meals and include additional fibre in the diet.
- Add some aloe vera juice to your daily intake of fluids to heal the intestinal lining.
- Papaya tablets can be taken after a meal as a digestive aid.
- Avoid heavy lifting. Should lifting be part of your occupation, avoid such exertion for several hours after meals.
- Place several inches of elevating blocks under the legs of the head of the bed. This will allow gravity to keep the stomach lower when sleeping.
- Do not lie down immediately after eating.
- Avoid spicy foods and fried foods. They delay digestion and prolong the emptying of the stomach.
- Avoid coffee, tea, alcohol, colas and cigarettes. Do not wear tight clothing.
- Avoid constipation and straining during bowel movements.

HICCUPS

They usually aren't painful but they can be annoying. Hiccups are more common in men and follow an irritation of the nerves that control the muscles used for breathing. Unless the hiccups are prolonged, they usually go away in a few hours on their own and are nothing to be concerned about.

- Treatments that focus on adjusting the level of carbon dioxide include holding one's breath, breathing into a paper bag, drinking a glass of water rapidly, and pulling the tongue forwards with the fingers.
- If you want a more novel approach, try eating one teaspoonful of dry sugar or gently inhaling a little pepper – enough to make you sneeze. Sneezing usually adjusts the spastic contractions of the diaphragm.

HIVES

They itch and show up as large, red blotchy areas on the skin.

The skin demonstrates its allergic reaction to something by presenting us with hives. Special cells release histamine and this makes blood vessels leak fluid into the deepest layers of the skin. The result: itchy wheals that may stay with you for hours or minutes and sometimes in the most annoying places.

- Over-the-counter antihistamines are good and they are found in cold and hay fever preparations – but watch out, they may make you sleepy.
- Cold compresses will take the swelling and itching down but it is only temporary. Try an ice-cube rubbed directly on the wheal.
- Calamine lotion will temporarily relieve the itching.
- Three tablespoonfuls of cornflour mixed with a tablespoonful of vinegar mixed into a paste and pressed on the hives will cool them down and hurry their disappearance.
- Take some time to track down the cause and then avoid it at all costs in the future. If it is something you can't avoid, take an antihistamine before exposure, if you can.

HIGH BLOOD PRESSURE

On a routine physical examination, your doctor tells you that you have high blood pressure – but just what does that mean?

When the heart pumps blood through the arteries, the blood presses against the walls of the blood vessels as it travels through them. Arteriosclerosis or hardening of the arteries is common in individuals with high blood pressure. Because the arteries are narrowed by the plaque deposited along them by cholesterol, it becomes more difficult for the blood to pass through these narrowed passageways. As a result, the blood must be forced through and this creates an increase in blood pressure.

Blood pressure is measured as the systolic pressure over the diastolic pressure. For instance, a blood pressure recorded as '120 over 80' would be classified as normal, according to the table below.

Millions have high blood pressure. It is defined as a systolic pressure (the pressure exerted by the blood when the heart is pumping) of 140 mm Hg or greater, or a diastolic pressure (the pressure in the vessels when the heart is at rest between beats, when the pressure on the arteries is at its lowest) of 90 mm Hg or greater.

High blood pressure is a major risk factor for cardiovascular disease because the heart must work harder to pump the blood, which can lead to heart failure or stroke.

Condition	Systolic (top number)	Diastolic (bottom number)	What to do
Normal	less than 130	less than 85	Check in 2 years
High-normal	130-139	85-89	Check in 1 year
Hypertension			
Stage 1	140-159	90-99	Check in 2 months
Stage 2	160-179	100-119	See doctor within 1 month
Stage 3	180-209	110-119	See doctor within week
Stage 4	210 or higher	120 or higher	See doctor immediately

Note: Blood pressure conditions are based on the average of two or more readings taken at two differing times.

All stages of hypertension are associated with an increased risk of non-fatal and fatal heart conditions, stroke and kidney disease.

Those with high blood pressure often have no symptoms at all. However, there are some warning signs such as headache, sweating, rapid pulse, shortness of breath, dizziness and some disturbances of vision – all as a result of the increased pressure on various vessels in the blood system.

Once diagnosed with high blood pressure, because there are few symptoms, it is important to stay on your medication and have your blood pressure taken regularly.

- Take the anti-hypertension medication prescribed by your doctor.
- Eliminate all salt from your diet. Salt retains fluid, which in turn increases

the pressure. Read food labels carefully for salt content. Some canned vegetables and certain commercially-prepared foods have high levels of salt. Some toothpastes and over-the-counter medications also have salt; soft drinks, preservatives, sugar substitutes, softened water and soy sauce are usually high in salt content. Salt may raise your blood pressure if you are sodium sensitive. Limit your daily intake to 2,300 mg.

- Eat a high-fibre diet. Oat bran, fruits and vegetables, such as apples, bananas, broccoli, cantaloup and green leafy vegetables. Avoid foods such as anchovies, chocolate, pickled products, pork, sausage and smoked or processed meats, such as hot dogs.
- Avoid over-exertion, particularly in hot weather.
- Lose excess pounds. Losing as few as 10 pounds may make a meaningful drop in blood pressure.
- Avoid alcohol. Alcohol may reduce your heart's pumping ability and cause resistance to blood pressure medication.
- Exercise. Regular, moderate activity, such as a 30-minute brisk walk three to five times a week, may help prevent and treat high blood pressure.
- Don't smoke.
- Manage stress.
- Both garlic and onions on a daily basis have been shown to have a good effect on blood pressure. Add them to salads and sandwiches.
- Eat several apples a day: the pectin in apples have been shown to help in reducing high blood pressure.
- Cucumbers are excellent natural diuretics and are an aid in lowering blood pressure.

HOT FLUSHES

One minute you're perfectly comfortable, the next you are so hot you can't stand it – the sweat is running down the back of your neck, your face is flushed and all you want to do is rip all your clothes off to get cool. You're having a hot flush.

As your body's oestrogen levels drop as you approach menopause, hot flushes can begin. Hot flushes are simply a symptom of menopause. This is the time in a woman's life when she stops ovulating. Most women experience this so-called 'change of life' at approximately age 50, although some do have this change in hormones earlier and a few later.

These hormonal changes create a disturbance in thermoregulation. The hypothalamus (the gland that serves as the body's thermostat) triggers a sudden, downward setting of the body's core temperature. In response to this cooling, blood vessels expand to increase the volume of blood flow, resulting in a measurably higher skin temperature and a hot flush that can last from a few seconds to a minute at a time.

This period of problematic thermoregulation usually lasts for about five years. At this time, oestrogen levels drop, although the hormone does not disappear entirely and other organs take over the production of oestrogen and other hormones.

The symptoms that accompany these hot flushes can include dizziness, headache, difficulty in breathing, heart palpitations and a depression which is part of the lowered oestrogen.

- Oestrogen replacement is effective in not only alleviating hot flushes, but also helping prevent the bone loss of osteoporosis.
- Progesterone supplementation will assist in the balance of hormones to prevent uterine cancer.
- Reduce stress where possible. Learn to relax.
- Include moderate exercise in your daily routine to reduce the burden on the adrenal glands.
- A well-balanced nutritious diet is mandatory.
- Avoid dairy products, sugar and red meat.
- Eliminate caffeine and alcohol.
- Add broccoli, kelp, salmon with the bones (for calcium) and sardines.
- Regular exercise, including some low-impact aerobics, will aid in the prevention of bone loss.
- Dryness in the vaginal area can be treated with vitamin E oil applied topically.
- Dress in layers so you can take something off when you begin to feel hot.
- Wear natural fibres as they give your body more ventilation and keep you cooler.
- Drink lots of water to aid in keeping your body temperature normal.

HYPERVENTILATION

Over-breathing, until you think you are having a heart attack, can be pretty frightening. Your fingers are tingling, your heart is pounding and your palms are sweaty. But it's not a heart attack, you have hyperventilated and caused your body to go into a panic reaction.

Most cases of hyperventilation are caused by anxiety. Fear causes you to over-breathe and you exhale large amounts of carbon dioxide, throwing your body into a metabolic tailspin.

- Breathing into a paper bag is an age-old remedy. It allows you to replace the carbon dioxide and get your body back into sync.
- Sit down, try to slow your breathing down and make a conscious effort to relax.
- If you experience this often, you need to eliminate caffeine and stimulants such as tea, cola drinks and chocolate from your diet.
- Also avoid nicotine, another stimulant.
- Episodes of hyperventilation usually last for half an hour but you need to learn to stop them by getting your breathing under control.

HYPNOSIS

You have panic attacks or irritable bowel syndrome and the doctor has told you that you need to 'relax'. Just how do you go about relaxing?

- One of the ways is to be trained in visualisation techniques through hypnosis or self-hypnosis.
- Hypnosis can be helpful in behaviour modification. For example, doctors sometimes recommend hypnosis as part of an overall smoking cessation treatment programme. Rather than put you to sleep, hypnosis leads to increased relaxation; you have a narrowed focus of attention and a heightened sense of suggestibility.
- The person who hypnotises you offers suggestions that help alter the way you react to specific situations.
- Hypnosis can be used to help people cope with pain, reduce anxiety and remember aspects of a stressful event.
- Hypnosis can have long- and short-term benefits.

Learning these visualisation and hypnosis techniques can help you cope with a variety of problems.

HYPOGLYCAEMIA (LOW BLOOD SUGAR)

All of a sudden you feel shaky, your skin is cool and damp and you are aware of a feeling of hunger. "If I don't get something to eat soon, I think I'm going to faint." You could be right, your body is telling you that your blood sugar has suddenly dropped.

The most common scenario occurs two to four hours after eating. A very rapid absorption of glucose into the circulation causes an outpouring of a corresponding excess of insulin. In some mild maturity-onset diabetic patients this may occur after a carbohydrate load and may be one of the first indications of diabetes mellitus.

Symptoms may include faintness, weakness, trembling, palpitations, diaphoresis, hunger and nervousness. This might be followed by headache, confusion, visual disturbances, and motor weakness, which can progress to loss of consciousness.

Low blood glucose (<40mg /100 ml) or low plasma glucose (<50mg/100 ml), along with specific complaints are necessary for the diagnosis of hypoglycaemia.

- Acute episodes of hypoglycaemia should be treated by giving glucose promptly. Stir 2 or 3 tablespoonfuls of granulated sugar into a glass of fruit juice or water.
- A correct diet is essential to correct hypoglycaemia. Remove all sugar, refined and processed foods such as instant rice, white flour, soft drinks, alcohol and salt. Avoid very sweet fruits and juices such as grapes and prune. Baked potatoes should be eaten plain or with a small amount of low-fat yoghurt to moisten. Include vegetables, brown rice, artichokes, seeds, nuts, and cottage cheese in your diet.
- Do not go without eating. Eat six to eight small meals throughout the day. It is better to 'graze' during the day than to eat one large meal and then go four or five hours without food until the next meal. A small snack of something high in fibre before bedtime will aid the hypoglycaemic to maintain a proper blood sugar level during the night until breakfast.
- A high-fibre diet will aid in avoiding blood sugar highs and lows. Fibre by itself, such as found in popcorn or rice bran, will slow down a hypoglycaemia reaction.
- Avoid caffeine, alcohol and smoking which contribute to extremes of blood sugar.

IMPOTENCE

She is the most exciting woman you've ever been with. You've waited for this night for so long. But ... unexpectedly you find yourself unable to perform.

Most men will experience a failure to achieve an erection at some time during their lives – but when it happens to you – it is devastating. The question goes through your mind, "Am I still a man?" True impotence is the inability to achieve or maintain an erection for more than several months at a time. A single experience of failure to maintain an erection is not impotence.

Causes can be vascular disease; diabetes (the primary medical cause); some medications; the use of drugs and alcohol, including nicotine.

Sexual function naturally decreases with age. The older man may require more stimulation and an increase in time that it takes for erection to take place.

- Take a look at your medications. More than 200 drugs have been identified as contributing to the problem.
- Avoid both alcohol and nicotine. Alcohol decreases the body's ability to produce testosterone (the major male hormone). Nicotine is a vasoconstrictor and since the penis is dependent entirely on the vascular system for erectile tissue to respond to stimulus, nicotine should be one of the first items to be removed in any treatment.
- Recreational drugs inhibit erections so you should avoid all of them.
- Try to relax and avoid being anxious about 'the next time'.
- Talk it over with your partner. Don't let a temporary lack of an erection ruin intimacy.
- Eat a healthy and balanced diet.
- Avoid hot baths and saunas.
- Avoid extreme exercise as it may reduce the production of male hormones.
- There is a long list of foods that are considered aphrodisiacs. If you want to try some, include pumpkin seeds and celery in your diet; they are both high in zinc.

INCONTINENCE

A leaky bladder with damp undergarments and your fear of the odour this causes can keep you housebound.

Urinary incontinence is a symptom, usually of lax muscle tone, not a disease. It can ruin your social life, if you let it.

- Temporarily cut down on your fluids, particularly before going to bed, but be sure you don't cut down enough to cause dehydration.
- Avoid alcohol as it relaxes the sphincter muscle that controls the bladder.
- Avoid caffeine and grapefruit juice, as they are well-known diuretics.
- Drink cranberry juice as it is acidic and low in ash and beneficial to the health of your bladder.
- Constipation can contribute to incontinence. When you strain to move your bowels you can weaken the bladder muscles.

- Stop smoking. Nicotine irritates the bladder.
- Keep your weight under control.
- Empty your bladder regularly. An over-full bladder has stretched walls and contributes to the inability to control the sphincter when you cough, laugh or sneeze.
- Practice Kegel exercises. When urinating, try to stop the flow and then restart. Once you have identified these muscles, practice the same exercise daily 100 times to strengthen the bladder sphincter.
- Be prepared. Wear an absorbent pad or undergarment while you retrain your sphincter muscle.

INDIGESTION

You feel just like you have swallowed a large balloon. Your belt is cutting you in half and you wish you could just belch and get rid of all that wind. You hope it is only indigestion and not something more serious.

Indigestion is a feeling of abdominal distention, a bloated feeling, belching, nausea, vomiting or a burning sensation after eating. Chewing with the mouth open or talking while chewing can cause air to be swallowed along with the food, which causes a bloated feeling. Fermentation of food in the colon can produce hydrogen and carbon dioxide gases which contribute to the feeling of indigestion. Carbohydrates are the main food source for gas because of the bacteria they contain.

If the feeling of indigestion is temporary, it should subside within a short time. However, this can often be a first symptom of a heart attack and should not be dismissed as 'only wind'.

- The person who has frequent bouts of indigestion needs to be aware of which foods cause the problem and stay away from those foods.
- Stress and a lack of digestive enzymes can also cause indigestion. Hydrochloric acid is necessary for the breakdown and digestion of foods.
- If taking a tablespoonful of apple cider vinegar relieves your indigestion, then you are lacking in this essential acid. You can purchase enzymes which increase hydrochloric acid at any health food store. If it increases the problem, then you already are too acidic. Do not take enzymes which contain hydrochloric acid.
- Teas of catnip, camomile, comfrey, goldenseal, fenugreek, papaya and peppermint are all beneficial.
- If the apple cider vinegar aided in relieving your symptoms, you can

continue to sip some with water during meals.
- Charcoal tablets can absorb gas but should only be used infrequently.
- Fibre-rich foods such as fresh fruit, vegetables and whole grains will be beneficial.
- Avoid refined carbohydrates, dairy products, caffeine, tomatoes, carbonated beverages, fried and fatty goods, spicy foods, red meat, beans.
- Limit the intake of peanuts and lentils as they inhibit digestive enzymes.
- Barley broth will decrease both bloating and heartburn.
- Exercise, both stretching and walking will increase the digestion and shorten the transit time for food through the intestine, decreasing the amount of time it has to ferment.
- Chew food thoroughly and do not talk with your mouth full to avoid swallowing air with the food.

INFERTILITY

You look around at all your friends, they have several children. Your mother's friends are beginning to ask pointed questions. So now you think maybe it's time you should have a baby.

Well, why haven't you become pregnant?

If there isn't some reproductive difficulty, then:
- Give yourself time. If you are under 30, you should be able to conceive within a year.
- Forget all the charts and scheduled sex. Just go ahead and make love when you feel like it. Let Nature take its course. It often works.
- Avoid stress. Your body often limits your fertility at such times.
- Remain lying down after intercourse. That will allow the sperm to travel up the reproductive road.
- Stop smoking. Nicotine impairs the fertility of both men and women.
- Test for ovulation. You can buy an over-the-counter kit which reads the levels of ovulation-releasing hormone in your urine.
- Keep your weight within normal levels. Fat produces oestrogen and too high or too low oestrogen can throw your reproductive hormones out of balance.
- Cut back on exercise. If you lose too much fat you will stop ovulating.
- Avoid douches. Douching interferes with the pH levels of the vagina, making it inhospitable to sperm.
- Limit caffeine. Caffeine seems to reduce reproductive abilities.

- Bad colds can reduce a man's sperm count. Give yourself time to recover.
- Some over-the-counter medications can reduce sperm count.
- Avoid hot baths and close-fitting underwear. They bring the testicles in contact with too much heat, reducing the sperm count.
- Excessive lovemaking can also reduce your sperm count. Give yourself a day or two to recover before you try again.

INFLUENZA

You ache all over, your head is throbbing, the light hurts your eyes and you have no interest in even getting out of bed. Feverish the one minute, chilled the next, you feel desperately fatigued with a loss of appetite. Groaning, you ask, "Did anyone see the truck that hit me?"

You have the flu.

Influenza is a highly contagious viral infection of the respiratory tract. It is spread by person-to-person contact and airborne droplet spray. Individual strains of the virus are constantly mutating and because of this, vaccines against influenza have been only partly successful.

Influenza appears suddenly after an incubation period from exposure to the virus of approximately one to three days. Symptoms are similar to the common cold – headache, weakness, aching of the arms, legs and back. The next symptom may be nausea and vomiting – the first indication that this is not merely a cold. Weakness, sweating and fatigue may persist for several days or occasionally for weeks.

Today influenza is rarely fatal – but in the elderly or the immune compromised individual – pneumonia can follow, as well as ear infections and other complications.

- There is no specific therapy. Non-exertion and a comfortable environment are the best remedies.
- Aspirin is not recommended unless the fever is high or the symptoms prevent sleep.
- If necessary a cough syrup can suppress the cough enough to allow you to rest.
- Get plenty of liquids and bed rest until you feel well enough to resume normal activities.
- Stay at home. Avoid spreading this highly contagious ailment.
- Eucalyptus oil in an inhaler can help overcome the feeling of congestion and ease breathing.

- A warm salt water gargle is soothing to a raspy throat.
- Lubricate your tender nose with K-Y jelly.
- Keep your feet warm. A pair of socks while you rest in bed may help you feel more comfortable.
- Eat lightly. Dry toast, bananas, apple purée, cottage cheese and baked potatoes are good choices until you feel better.
- Individuals who have chronic illnesses, particularly those such as chronic bronchitis, should have an annual flu injection from their doctor. The elderly, whose immune system is naturally decreasing, should also consider an annual flu injection.
- Avoidance of those individuals who are already sick – and careful, thorough handwashing are good preventative measures.
- During the flu and cold season, always wash your hands before touching your face, particularly in the areas of the nose and eyes.

INGROWN TOENAIL

You can't even get a shoe on without pain. It feels like a wrestler just stomped on your toe.

An ingrown nail occurs when the toenail – usually on a big toe – grows into the soft tissue at the side of the nail.

You need to assist the nail to grow out over the skin fold.

- Soak your foot in warm water to soften the nail. Dry and then insert a tiny wisp of sterile cotton between the edge of the nail and the toe. This cotton will lift the nail so it can grow past this painful tissue. Change the cotton daily until the nail has grown out.
- Apply some antiseptic to the painful tissue, particularly if it is inflamed.
- Avoid pointed toe shoes or shoes that are too tight. They not only add to the problem, they probably are the cause of the problem.
- Never cut your toenails too short. Cut straight across with a nail-clipper made specifically for toenails.
- Watch for infection. An infection in the feet can lead to more serious problems, particularly for diabetics.

INSECT STINGS

Those pesky bugs buzzing around your head and sometimes landing on your skin, biting and causing itching and reddened skin. Most insect stings simply itch and produce a small welt that disappears in a few days.

The problems created by the sting of an insect are caused by the injection of the venom of the insect into the skin. Some insect bites are quite harmless, such as the bite of midges or fleas. However, ticks and mosquitoes can carry such diseases as Lyme disease, spotted fever or malaria.

Bees, wasps, hornets and ants cause an allergic reaction in some sensitive individuals. These allergic reactions are often severe and sometimes fatal. The symptoms are difficulty in swallowing, hoarseness, laboured breathing, weakness, severe swelling and feeling of impending doom.

- For ant, mosquito, midge and flea bites, wash the area thoroughly with soap and water and apply a paste made of baking soda and water, or a little dab of toothpaste.
- Ticks should be removed immediately with tweezers: try to remove the entire creature without leaving any of it in the skin. Scrub the area with soap and water.
- Bee, wasp and hornet stingers should be removed by scraping against the stinger, in the same direction in which it was inserted, with a firm scraper (such as the edge of a credit card). Anyone with a known allergy to these insects should obtain an emergency treatment kit from their doctor.
- Calamine lotion can aid in relieving itching, as can a poultice of cornflour and witch-hazel.
- Brewer's yeast (which is high in B vitamins) and garlic can be taken orally or rubbed on the skin. Insects have tiny antennae which aid them in seeking a host animal and they are repelled by both of these natural foods.
- Wear plain, light-coloured clothing – avoid clothing that appears flowery. Insects can be attracted to perfume, hairspray and shiny jewellery. Cover your feet when walking through grass or bushes.
- Avoid alcohol as this causes the blood vessels to dilate, bringing more blood to the surface and attracting mosquitoes and some flies.

INSOMNIA

You lie in bed exhausted. Your mind is racing, you toss and turn and pound the pillow. It's 3 am and you still can't get to sleep. A quick glance at the alarm clock tells you it will soon be time to get up. You curse and turn over again, praying for sleep.

You are not alone, millions are troubled nightly by insomnia.

Some people need only three hours sleep a night. Others are unproductive and irritable unless they get a full 10 hours. Your personal need for sleep remains surprisingly the same throughout most of your lifetime.

Transient insomnia is when you have slept badly for a few days. Short-term insomnia is sleeping badly for up to three weeks. Chronic insomnia means poor sleep has troubled you for months or even years. Chronic insomnia follows one of two patterns. You either have trouble falling asleep, or you fall asleep easily but have trouble staying asleep.

More than 50 per cent of people with chronic insomnia have psychological stress. Depression, anxiety, worries about children, finances, marriage – all can create insomnia.

- Begin by keeping a sleep log on how you sleep and what you do during the day. Then change something and log your sleep again. For example, if you typically nap during the day, cut it out and see if your sleep improves.
- Eliminate caffeine.
- Many medications can cause sleep problems. Check with your doctor to see if this is the reason for your sleeplessness.
- Reduce the time you spend in bed – too much time in bed can cause shallow sleep.
- Create a restful environment – make the bedroom a place for sleeping – not where you do office chores, balance your cheque-book, or solve other problems.
- Deal with worries before bedtime – write down primary worries and outline solutions. Once you identify some solutions, you will be less inclined to fret over the problem.
- Decide on the amount of sleep you need – establish a bedtime to get the proper amount of sleep.
- Avoid clock-watching – if there is a clock by the bed, put it out of sight when you go to bed for the night.
- Have a healthy bedtime snack – try a small glass of milk or a banana. People always sleep better if they don't go to bed hungry.
- Avoid caffeine after the evening meal – late-night caffeine is responsible for many restless nights.
- Shun tobacco – nicotine can contribute to shallow sleeping.
- Relax – don't try to attain sleep. Relax and let Nature take over. If sleep doesn't come, read a book, get out of bed for half an hour and do some small chore before going back to bed.
- Older individuals sleep less soundly, with more awakenings during the

night. Sometimes having many brief awakenings gives you the impression that you've been up all night.

- Cutting down on daytime naps and keeping involved and busy often means a better night's sleep for older people.
- Melatonin is a naturally-occurring hormone that can act as a natural sleep aid and can be purchased at a health food shop.
- Most people can overcome insomnia by effectively addressing the cause of poor sleep with self-help measures.

INTERMITTENT CLAUDICATION

You get pain in the calf of your leg when you walk. Other than that, you feel just fine.

Known as intermittent claudication it is to your extremities what a heart attack is to the heart. That is, a symptom of vascular disease. You have restricted blood flow to the arms and the legs.

- Stop smoking. This is such a major factor in the disease that you must stop before any other remedy will work.
- Walk. This is the best exercise for this ailment.
- Protect and care for your feet. Even a small sore can turn into a large ulcer in feet and legs with limitations of circulation.
- Lose weight. Unburden those aching legs and feet.
- Avoid using a heating pad. No matter how cold your feet feel, you can cause a serious burn with a heating pad. Warm your feet with wool socks.
- Have your doctor check your blood pressure and your cholesterol. These are additional risk factors that you should be aware of.

IRRITABLE BOWEL SYNDROME

There are grumpy, irritable people and grumpy, irritable bowels. You can have a grumpy irritable bowel without being a grumpy, irritable person – it means that certain foods, drinks and stressful events give you alternating bouts of diarrhoea, constipation and abdominal pain.

A major factor in relieving symptoms is to pay attention to your eating habits.

- If something seems to irritate the condition, eliminate it from your diet.
- Eat on a regular schedule, don't overeat and don't eat on the run. Urgency and overeating can aggravate bowel irregularity.
- Add fibre to your diet – it helps prevent constipation. Include muesli,

crispbread, and whole grains. Because fibre can cause gas, add it gradually.
- Avoid substances that irritate the bowel – common irritants include tobacco, alcohol (beer and wine are the worst for people with IBS), caffeine, spicy foods, concentrated fruit juices, raw fruits or vegetables. Avoid fatty foods – they stimulate your bowels more than any other food.
- Limit dairy products – milk can cause abdominal cramping, gas and diarrhoea.
- Avoid dietetic sweeteners – they can cause diarrhoea.
- Drink six to eight glasses of water a day.
- Cut out fat as it is a stimulus to colonic contractions.
- Avoid spicy foods.
- Stop smoking.
- Use a hot water bottle or heating pad on your tummy.
- Participate in tension-relieving activities – sports, hobbies or regular physical exercise.

JET LAG

You've waited all year for your holiday. You have finally arrived at your hotel for your dream trip. The palm trees are waving, the beach is just a few feet away – and not only can you hardly stay awake, you are having trouble concentrating, you feel very irritable, you have diarrhoea and a roaring headache! Some holiday! It is only temporary, you have jet lag.

The more time zones you cross, the worse the jet lag will be.
- Before you leave, live on a sensible schedule for a couple of weeks.
- Get enough sleep before you leave.
- Fly during the day so you will arrive at night if you can. Have a light meal and go to bed. You'll feel a lot better in the morning.
- Don't drink alcohol on your flight. You'll arrive dehydrated.
- Drink plenty of fluids – airline cabins just suck the moisture out of your body so you need to replenish it regularly.
- Don't nap at your destination, you will only delay your time-zone adjustment.
- Keep to your regular exercise routine. Whatever you do at home, try to duplicate it at your holiday destination.
- Try to avoid making any important decisions when you first arrive and be sure that you watch your luggage and your wallet. Thieves know about

jet-lag inattention and are quick to capitalise on the unwary.
- Prepare for your return trip. Jet lag isn't over when you get home, it has just gone into reverse.

KIDNEY STONES

Grown men cry, other's beat their heads against the wall because of the pain. Mothers who have endured long labours before childbirth say, "There is nothing that hurts like a kidney stone."

A kidney stone is a hardened mineral deposit. It begins as a microscopic particle and grows slowly, developing into a stone over a period of months. You are more likely to form a stone when you are dehydrated.

Stones frequently remain undiagnosed until they begin to pass, causing a type of pain called renal colic.
- Avoid foods that contain or produce oxalic acid, such as asparagus, beets, parsley, rhubarb, sorrel, Swiss chard and vegetables of the cabbage family.
- Increase fluid intake and make the effort daily to drink at least 8 to 10 glasses of water. Other fluids do not count and some of them, such as alcohol and caffeine, contribute to the problem of stone formation.
- Limit dairy products and antacids.
- Reduce salt intake.
- Eat lots of water melon, a natural diuretic.
- Limit intake of animal protein and increase cereal and vegetable intake. High fibre aids in binding the calcium and oxalate for normal secretion.
- A daily 10 mg of magnesium seems to decrease the formation of stones.
- Exercise to keep the calcium mobilised in your bloodstream.
- For those prone to form stones, limit your vitamin C to no more than 3 grams daily.

KNEE PAIN

Your knees were not designed to twist and turn, kneeling and squatting all day long. Soccer players, carpenters, plumbers and housewives are just some of the people susceptible to knee pain and injury.

The knee joint is the largest joint in your body and one of the most complex. This structure of muscles, bones, ligaments and cartilage, supports and stabilises your knee as you bend, straighten and twist during daily activities.

- Watch your weight. For every pound you are overweight, you put an additional six pounds of stress on your knees.
- Over-the-counter painkillers are good to reduce inflammation and make you more comfortable.
- Some over-the-counter heat rubs can also aid in making the knee more comfortable.
- Strengthen the knee with exercises that build up the supporting muscles.
- Protect the knee to prevent further injury. Use an elastic wrap to immobilise the knee temporarily. Try walking with a cane in the hand opposite your painful knee for a few days. This reduces the weight-bearing forces by approximately 50 per cent.
- Rest. Avoid activities that cause pain, swelling or discomfort. Squatting, kneeling or walking up and down steep stairs or hills causes you to place weight on your bent knees.
- Ice-cold is preferable to heat in the beginning of an injury because it reduces swelling, inflammation and speeds healing. In the first three days of pain, apply ice wrapped in a cloth for no more than 20 minutes several times a day.
- Heat is best for chronic pain. It can also help relieve stiffness and prepare your muscles for strengthening exercises.
- Elevate your knee above the level of your heart whenever possible.
- Select the proper shoes for your activities. If you play a sport, pick the appropriate shoes and be sure they are in good condition.
- Stretch. Warm up and cool down properly before any athletic activities.

LACTOSE INTOLERANCE

You'd love to eat ice-cream but you know it will just make you sick. The same goes for a cheese pizza and cream cheese in a sandwich. Lactose intolerance makes anything made with milk give you enough gas to power a small car.

Your small intestine doesn't produce sufficient amounts of lactase, an enzyme you need to digest lactose, the natural sugar found in dairy products. Most adults after age 20 suffer from some degree of lactose intolerance.

- Limit your dairy products. You may be able to have some of your favourites a few times a week without difficulty.
- Supplement your diet with calcium. Eat sardines with the bones, spinach or broccoli.

- If you do drink milk, be sure to take it with other foods.
- Try yoghurt. It doesn't have the same lactose content of milk but use non-fat or low-fat yoghurt.
- Try an over-the-counter lactase enzyme.
- Experiment with cheese, some have less lactose than others, such as Swiss or Cheddar.
- Lactose is used as a filler in some medications. If you have difficulty, read labels or ask your pharmacist about your medications.

LARYNGITIS

You sound like a frog. Your throat is scratchy and it hurts to swallow. Finally, you end up talking in a husky whisper. Others might tell you that you sound sexy, but with such a sore throat you certainly don't feel very sexy.

When your vocal cords are swollen from overuse or from a virus, it is laryngitis.

- Be quiet. Give your vocal cords a rest.
- Use a cold-air humidifier to keep your throat moist.
- Use a steam vaporiser to restore the moisture.
- Drink lots of fluids. Try tea with honey or lemon, a soothing drink often used by professional singers.
- Breathe through your nose, not your mouth. Your nose is a natural humidifier.
- Stop smoking. Smoking dries out the throat.
- If you want to use cough drops, use fruit- or honey-flavoured ones and avoid the mint and mentholated ones.
- If you suffer from laryngitis often, consider voice training with a professional.

LAUGHTER

'Laughter is the best medicine.' We have all heard that expression but now medical science tells us that laughter can lower blood pressure, promote circulation, stimulate digestion and reduce pain.

If you find that your sense of humour is slipping, take that as a clue that you may be slipping into something more serious.

- Brighten your outlook by focusing on the silly behaviour of others.
- Read or listen to something funny daily; it will help you lighten your load.

- Laugh out loud when you can, as it is good for your muscles.
- When you are angry at a co-worker or a pompous person imagine them naked – that ought to get you laughing.
- Use humour in your business world when you can, as it often helps to sell ideas.
- Avoid mean jokes; they are unproductive.
- Laugh at yourself. No one knows as well as you just how silly you can be at times.

LUMBAGO

(See *Back Pain*)

LUMP IN THE THROAT

You keep swallowing, trying to move that little ball in your throat. No matter how much you try, it is still there, so you swallow again and again, beginning to feel a little panicky. It is still there even after you drink something, clear your throat or swallow hard.

Known medically as globus, many things cause this uncomfortable feeling. The small muscular opening in the lower part of the throat becomes tense. The tension in the throat tells your brain something is lodged there, even when nothing is.

Many things can cause this uncomfortable feeling:
- Stress, anxiety and depression.
- Medications for high blood pressure or depression.
- Antihistamines.
- A recent cough or cold.
- A hiatus hernia.
- Being overweight.
- Acid indigestion, particularly when caused by the overeating of fatty foods or chocolate.

If there is no medical cause, you might try:
- Changing medications.
- Drinking at least eight glasses of water a day.
- Using a nasal spray filled with warm salt water.
- Chewing sugarless gum or sucking on lozenges that stimulate saliva.
- Avoid heartburn. Don't go to bed on a full stomach.

- Avoid alcohol, chocolate and fatty meals.
- Lose weight if you need to.

MEMORY IMPROVEMENT

You can't find your car keys – and you're late for an appointment. You see a friend in the supermarket and can't remember her name. You think, "I'm going senile, I can't remember anything anymore!"

Simple forgetfulness isn't a disease. Aging doesn't affect short-term memory. However, long-term memory sometimes declines with age. To store and retrieve information from memory, your brain performs a complex chain of chemical and electrical functions involving nerve cells. As you age, some of these cells may deteriorate and function less efficiently.

Memory can decline for a variety of reasons, including depression, medical illnesses and the side-effects of drugs. Normal forgetfulness can be caused by getting lazy about using the memory.

However, memory lapses that become more frequent and severe should be cause for concern.

- Tune up your memory – get busy and realign those brain cells.
- Get organised. Manage daily activities with routine.
- Stretch your mental muscles. Try crossword puzzles, play bridge or other games to sharpen your concentration.
- Use lists. Don't bother to memorise things you can list on paper.
- Make associations. Find ways to cue your memory. Use mnemonic cues to recall things by association.
- Practice. Practice paying attention. When you are introduced to someone, listen carefully and repeat the person's name. At parties, take an inventory of people you see, rehearse names in your mind.
- Try not to worry. Fretting about memory can lead to more forgetfulness, especially if you are tired or under stress.

MÉNIÈRE'S DISEASE

You are suddenly dizzy, you can't hear and there is a ringing in your ears. You feel nauseated and sometimes feel so sick you have to vomit. Ménière's disease has struck.

The cause is unknown but the dizziness can appear suddenly and last up to 24 hours.

- Since allergies (which can cause fluid retention) with watery eyes and runny nose, can be a part of the problem, an antihistamine can reduce the pressure in the ear.
- Reduced sodium intake, particularly for women during the premenstrual period, can be beneficial.
- Over-the-counter medications for travel sickness may help.
- Avoid caffeine, salt, sugar and alcohol as they all raise blood pressure and increase fluid to the ear.
- Stop smoking. Nicotine decreases the size of blood vessels and increases blood pressure.
- Be calm: these attacks usually only last for one day.

MENOPAUSE

(See *Hot Flushes*)

MENSTRUAL CRAMPS

Your abdomen feels like you swallowed a football and the pain is intense. It is time for your period and you know you have to suffer from menstrual cramps until your flow gets started. Menstrual cramps often accompany menstruation.

Prostaglandins, hormone-like substances that are produced in the body have an incredible range of physiological effects. Prostaglandins, released just prior to menstruation, cause the uterus to go into spasms, which can be painful. Women who have the most severe cramps have a higher level of prostaglandins in their menstrual blood.

These cramps are often accompanied with water retention, skin eruptions, headaches, bloating of the abdomen, backache, breast swelling and tenderness, insomnia, fatigue, nervousness, joint pain, fainting and personality changes such as outbursts of irritability or anger.

- Sip a hot drink and sit in a hot bath. Heat promotes blood flow, easing the pain. Some women achieve the same effect by lying back with a covered hot water bottle or heating pad against the stomach.
- Mild exercise, aimed at strengthening the abdominal muscles, as well as relieving the stress that can accompany the cramps, is beneficial.
- Relaxation techniques, including the same breathing techniques used in natural childbirth, can also be helpful.

- Regular exercise that will improve circulation – jogging, walking, swimming and cycling – to bring more oxygen to the blood, will aid in relaxing the uterus.
- Do not use salt, caffeine, alcohol, dairy products, sugar or red meat as they all contribute to the fluid retention and bloating.
- A healthy diet will aid in relieving depression. Increase water consumption to aid in reducing fluid retention.
- Avoid diuretics because they rob you of essential minerals.

MIGRAINE

There are bright flashes of lights before your eyes, you are overcome with nausea – just when you are getting ready to go to work – and you know a migraine headache has struck. You have no choice, you just have to phone in sick and go to bed in a darkened room. Migraine is a severe, recurring headache, with or without associated visual and gastrointestinal disturbance. The cause of migraine is unknown but it has been suggested that a functional disturbance in the circulation to the head is involved.

These headaches may be preceded by a short period of depression, irritability, restlessness or lack of appetite, and in some by scintillating areas of light in the field of vision.

- Try avoiding some of the foods that have been associated with migraines: milk and other dairy products, chocolate, cola drinks, onions, pork, eggs, citrus fruits, wheat, coffee and alcohol, aged cheese, pickled herring.
- Avoid common food additives: monosodium glutamate and nitrites. Read the labels carefully. Monosodium glutamate can be present in any processed food and nitrites are found in hot dogs, bacon, ham and salami.
- Fluctuating oestrogen can also be a cause – discontinuing supplemental oestrogen (including oral contraceptives) should be considered.
- Aspirin may alleviate mild attacks.
- Allergies are a common cause of migraine and these should be considered in any diagnosis.
- Constipation, stress and lack of exercise can all contribute to the difficulty.
- Hypoglycaemia can often be the cause. Appropriate diet may end the suffering. Individuals with varying levels of glucose intolerance who are given a high-protein, low-carbohydrate, low-sugar diet, with meals spread out to six times a day should find improvement within 90 days.

- Regular aerobic exercise can greatly reduce the incidence of migraines.
- Alternating cold and hot showers have been shown to stop migraines for many patients.
- Biofeedback training can lessen the severity of the pain.
- Avoid salt, fried foods and sugar.

MORNING SICKNESS

You thought of yourself as a serene Madonna – instead, you are throwing up as soon as you get up in the morning. Your eyes are watery, your hair is stringy and you really don't care. Nobody told you having a baby was going to be like this!

'Morning sickness' unfortunately, can happen at any time of the day – or night. Typically, morning sickness begins about the sixth week of pregnancy when the placenta begins to produce a special pregnancy hormone. Thankfully, most women feel better by week 8 to 13.

- Avoid fried, fatty foods. Your body takes longer to digest fats.
- Eat small meals, including fruit sugars such as grapes and juice – it will keep your blood sugar stable.
- Keep something at the bedside because moving with an empty stomach increases nausea. Eat some plain crackers before you even think about getting up in the morning.
- Drink lots of water to keep your electrolytes in balance.
- Sip ginger ale. It will aid in settling your stomach.
- A cup of camomile tea will also settle your stomach.
- Keep calm. The sickness will pass and you will feel better.

MORTON'S NEUROMA

You feel like there is an electric shock to the bottom of your foot and then your toes begin to sting or burn. You take off your shoe looking for a pebble but nothing is there. Morton's neuroma may be causing the trouble.

There is a growth of soft tissue on a nerve in the foot, usually the nerve between your third and fourth toes.

- Wear comfortable and well-fitting shoes, sandals or slippers.
- Try walking barefoot as often as possible.
- Sometimes a shoe support at the ball of the foot will help.

MOUTH ULCERS

Those little tiny ulcers inside your mouth that make everything you eat so painful – why do some people get them and not others? Nobody seems to know, but they do seem to be related to bad habits (like cheek biting), heredity, some food allergies, over-enthusiastic wielding of the toothbrush and emotional stress.

They can last from 4 to 20 days and make eating and drinking painful.

- Yoghurt (with active cultures) to fight the bacteria and cottage cheese to neutralise mouth acids can be applied directly to the lesion to reduce the pain.
- Avoid chewing-gum, mouthwash, coffee and any foods that you know can trigger an attack.
- Eat salads with lots of onions and garlic, Nature's own antibiotics.
- Dampen a black tea bag and apply to the ulcer. It contains tannin, an astringent that has good pain-relieving ability.
- Dilute 1 tablespoonful of hydrogen peroxide in a glass of water and swish it around your mouth to disinfect the ulcer and speed its healing.
- Swish some milk of magnesia around in your mouth. It will cover the ulcer and protect it from the food you eat while it heals.

MULTIPLE SCLEROSIS

One of the first indications of MS is a slight weakness in some muscle, but other than that the person feels well. As time goes on, coordination decreases.

Multiple sclerosis is caused by deterioration of the myelin sheath which covers the nerves. Scar tissue gathers where this protective sheath used to be. The cause is unknown and at present there is no cure, but living with the disease can be made easier.

- Rest, give nerves and muscles time to recover from any effort.
- Minimise stress as it aggravates symptoms.
- Avoid hot showers or baths. Cool baths or swimming in an unheated pool may improve symptoms.
- Maintain a normal routine.
- Try massage, as it improves and maintains muscle tone.
- Exercise gently, to improve muscle tone.
- Follow your doctor's instructions and take your prescribed medications.

MUSCLE CRAMPS

You were sound asleep and suddenly a cramp in your leg brought you upright, grasping your calf in pain.

Cramping often occurs after an individual has sweated profusely, usually after heavy muscular work, causing a loss of body fluids, affecting the body's electrolytes. Although muscle cramps can occur anywhere, most muscle cramps occur at night while in bed and usually affect the legs, particularly the muscles of the calf, and the feet. These kinds of cramps occur more frequently in the elderly, the young and individuals who suffer from arteriosclerosis.

If cramping occurs after walking and is relieved when you stop, this is an indication of intermittent claudication and you should see your doctor.

- Stand on a cold floor.
- Drinking fluids, with a calcium and magnesium tablet under your tongue, may correct the problem within a few minutes.
- Massage of the knotted area and the application of heat will also help the muscle relax.
- Regular exercise with stretching will help to keep the muscles properly toned and elongated.

MUSCLE PAIN

You are a weekend warrior: bowling, cycling, tennis, swimming. And then during the week, it's back to work. You consider yourself fit, but sometimes you can hardly get out of bed on Monday morning. Every muscle in your body is aching.

Whenever you exercise, you injure your muscles slightly. It takes 48 hours for muscles to recover.

- Use an ice-pack for 20 minutes.
- Remove the ice-pack and wrap the swollen muscle in an elastic bandage.
- Put your feet up, particularly if the sore muscle is in the leg.
- Rest for 24 hours, after which you may use heat to bring blood to the injured muscle.
- Stretch. Gradually stretching the muscle out will cause it to relax and give it a chance to heal.
- Massage the sore area gently.
- Exercise the next day, but very gently. It will help to work out some of the soreness.

- Take an over-the-counter anti-inflammatory. It may ease the soreness and make it easier to move again.
- Work on strength. Weak muscles could be part of the problem.

NAIL DIFFICULTIES

Nails protect the fingertips from injury. They are composed of protein, keratin and sulphur and grow approximately .05 to 1.2 mm a week. They can be stimulated to grow faster by tapping, such as typing or playing the piano regularly.

Nail changes or abnormalities are often the result of specific conditions, such as psoriasis, or nutritional deficiencies.

Doctors can often make a preliminary diagnosis of bodily ailments from the condition of the nails. Some of these signs are:

- Thick nails – difficulties with the vascular system.
- Lengthwise grooves or ridges – kidney disorders.
- Blue moons – lung disease.
- Brittle nails – thyroid disease, impaired kidney function or circulatory disease.
- Flat nails – indicate Raynaud's disease.
- Yellow nails – respiratory disorders, diabetes and liver disease.
- Dark nails – indicate anaemia.
- Nail beading – indicates rheumatoid arthritis.
- Pitted nails – a sign of psoriasis.
- Lack of moon – an overactive thyroid.
- Thinning nails – a sign of a skin disease.
- Nails separated from the nail bed – a thyroid disorder.
- Downward curved nail ends – heart, liver or lung disease.
- White lines – heart disease.
- White nails that are pink at the tip – a sign of cirrhosis.

Nutritional deficiencies can cause the following:

- Dryness and brittleness – lack of vitamin A.
- Ridges – lack of vitamin B.
- Excessive dryness and claw-like, rounded nails which curve over the ends of the fingers – lack of vitamin B12.
- Hangnails – lack of protein, folic acid and vitamin C.
- Fungus nails – lack of friendly bacteria.
- Splitting nails – lack of hydrochloric acid.

- Spoon nails and vertical ridges – lack of iron.
- Chipped, peeling or cracked nails – protein deficiency.

Here are some tips for relieving nail problems:

- Replace the lacking nutrient.
- Keep the hands out of water as much as possible and apply hand lotion to hands and around nail beds after immersion in water.
- Avoid harsh chemicals. Wear gloves when working with any products that are detrimental to the nails.
- If wearing false nails, they should be removed for a period of time to allow the nail to breathe and rest.
- During manicures, push the cuticle back into place very gently while damp, as the cuticle protects the nail bed and is a guard against bacteria entering the nail bed.

NAUSEA

Is there a person who hasn't said, "Oh, just thinking about that makes me sick!"

The sight of blood, the odours in hospital corridors, greasy food, a hair in your sandwich, changing a nappy on somebody else's baby – the list is endless.

It is a good idea to have something on hand when your tummy is not doing too well.

- Drink some luke-warm ginger ale, preferably after the fizz is gone.
- Eat some plain crackers or dry toast.
- Get some fresh air. A change of scene can do wonders for nausea.
- Lie down and lie still with your eyes closed.

NECK PAIN

We all know that the boss is a pain-in-the-neck, but a REAL pain in the neck can be even worse.

Some individuals are more at risk than others. If your work requires you to stay in a bent-over position or your desk is the wrong height, you could be heading for neck trouble.

- Apply ice at the end of the day for about 20 minutes while you relax.
- Over-the-counter anti-inflammatories such as aspirin or ibuprofen can reduce pain and inflammation.
- Get a chair that supports you properly with correct posture.

- A small towel rolled up and placed in the small of your back will aid in aligning your spine and give you additional support.
- Get up and walk around, swing your arms and give your neck a rest.
- Keep your head level with your chin pulled in.
- If you work at a computer, adjust your seat so that the screen is at eye level. Forcing yourself to look either up or down can cause your neck muscles to spasm.
- Sleep on a correct mattress and don't sleep on your stomach with your head turned to one side.
- Try a firm pillow to give your neck proper alignment and support.
- If the weather is damp and cold, wear a scarf. Muscles already strained can be worsened by contracting in cold weather.
- Learn some relaxation techniques and use them throughout the day.

NERVOUSNESS

(See *Anxiety*)

NIGHT-BLINDNESS

As you feel for your way to find your seat in a darkened theatre, you know what it feels like to have night-blindness. If you still can't see after about five minutes, then perhaps you have reason for concern, particularly if you drove to get there.

- Increase your vitamin A – see your doctor for the correct dosage.
- Clean off the windscreen and headlights to give yourself as much visibility advantage as possible.
- Slow down – you can react to unexpected hazards more easily if you aren't going too fast.
- If the weather is really bad, with fog and rain or sleet, pull off to the side of the road and wait for better visibility.
- If night-blindness becomes a serious problem, leave early enough to be sure you only drive in the daytime, or ask somebody else to do the driving.

NOSEBLEED

You walked into the door going to the bathroom in the middle of the night and you can't believe how much your nose can bleed.

- Plug the bleeding side with cotton moistened with an over-the-counter decongestant. If you don't have any, white vinegar will do.

- After plugging, pinch your nose, applying continuous pressure for six or seven minutes. Leave the plug in for another 20 minutes.
- Sit up straight. If you put your head back you will swallow blood.
- Try an ice-pack at the bridge of the nose to narrow the blood vessels.
- Control high blood pressure.
- Keep the inside of your nose moist with K-Y jelly during the winter months.
- Keep the air in your home moisturised with a humidifier.
- Take 500 mg of vitamin C daily to aid in the formation of collagen.
- Once the bleeding is stopped, refrain from any activity for several hours and vigorous exercise for several days.
- When bleeding is controlled, apply a small amount of vitamin E inside the nose and pack with gauze.

OBESITY

You go to buy a new outfit and you can't believe it, you take a size larger than you did the last time. Or you are looking forward to the big dance but last year's suit is too small? You finally decide, you really MUST do something about your weight.

Take in more calories than your body needs and it stores it as fat, it is as simple as that. The capacity of the body to store protein and carbohydrate is limited, and excess food is converted into fat and stored.

Obesity is manageable. Goals must be realistic and you must be prepared to change dietary patterns for life. You must have the desire to change your lifestyle.

3,500 calories equals 1 pound of fat. In order to lose 1 pound you must either reduce caloric intake by 3,500 calories or increase physical activity to burn 3,500 calories.

- Learn the calorie content and the fat content of the foods you eat in order to control intake.
- Purchase a cookbook that specialises in low-fat cooking so that you can eat your favourite foods with reduced fat content. Diets don't work if you are unable to eat some of your favourite foods.
- Begin an exercise programme. Exercise is the best way to control your weight, rather than strictly controlling calories – while maintaining good skin and muscle tone.

- Regular walking can be sufficient exercise if you walk briskly and for more than 30 minutes at a time.
- Vary your exercise routine so it doesn't become monotonous. If you enjoy swimming, swim. If you enjoy cycling, then go for a bicycle ride. If you like to dance, dance along with the television or the radio while you do your household chores.
- Increase fibre intake with fruits and vegetables. Fibre provides bulk which will make you feel full longer.
- Do not weigh yourself more than once a week. Weight will fluctuate with hormonal changes and fluid retention.
- Drink six to eight glasses of water daily.
- Be aware of your weight. Let the waistline of your clothing tell you when you are putting on a few pounds. As soon as your clothes feel tighter, step up your exercise programme.
- Put less food on your plate and use smaller plates. A smaller plate will make it appear that you have more to eat.
- Do not let others control your food intake. Be prepared with answers for the person who wants you to "just try this cake, I made it myself".
- Include complex carbohydrates in your daily food plan.
- Avoid sweets, pastries, pies, cakes and doughnuts.
- Do not go food shopping on an empty stomach. You will be tempted to buy things you shouldn't.
- Take a list with you that you have prepared beforehand and only shop from that list.
- If you must have snack foods in the house for others or children, keep them in opaque containers and put them out of sight so you will not be triggered into eating something on impulse.
- Avoid food commercials on television. Leave the room or change channels.
- Have healthy snacks such as celery and carrot sticks on hand should you feel tempted to snack at other than meal times.
- Reward yourself for appropriate behaviour with something other than food. A small gift of clothing or something you enjoy, such as a book or a CD.

OEDEMA

Oedema is the accumulation of excess fluid in the body, usually in the feet and ankles. Persistent oedema may have a serious cause such as kidney, heart or liver disease. Temporary oedema may result from the intake of salty foods and usually will resolve itself in a few days.

Many mistakenly believe that the answer to oedema is to decrease their fluid intake when, in fact, the exact opposite is true. Increased fluid intake is necessary to flush the water-retaining salt from the cells.

- Increase fluid intake, reduce salt.
- Increase exercise, such as walking which will help the fluid move from the feet and legs.
- Avoid caffeine, fried foods, soy sauce, pickles, olives, dairy products, gravy, white sugar, chocolate, alcohol and smoking.
- Alfalfa or parsley tea will aid in the removal of fluid from the body tissues.

OILY SKIN

Your face shines brightly, even though you powder it several times a day. Your nose gleams like a beacon and when you run your fingers along the side of it, they come away covered with a fine film of oil.

Oily skin is genetic and your hormones are central to the kind of skin you will have. Pregnancy and some birth control pills can make your oil glands go haywire.

- Use a clay or mud mask, as it will absorb excess oil temporarily.
- Wash regularly with hot water and a good soap. But don't scrub, you will only stimulate the oil glands.
- After washing, use a toner to return your skin to its proper pH.
- Select cosmetics that are water-based, not oil-based.
- Apply powder over your entire face to set your make-up and absorb oil during the day.

OSTEOPOROSIS

You've seen them, the old ladies with a dowager's hump at the back of their neck. Or you heard about someone's auntie who slipped on the rug and broke her hip. Anyone can get osteoporosis but women are more likely to get it than men.

- Exercise – it can actually increase bone mass.
- Take in sufficient calcium: you need 1,500 mg daily. Low-fat cheese, yoghurt, salmon, sardines and nuts are good sources. Fortify other foods with non-fat dry milk.

- Avoid caffeine as it aids in the excretion of minerals.
- Avoid cola drinks as they contain phosphoric acid which interferes with the absorption of calcium.
- Supplemental oestrogen, where appropriate, will aid in the assimilation of calcium.
- Get sufficient vitamin D. A minimum of 800 IU daily if you don't get sufficient sunshine.
- Avoid alcohol, as it reduces bone formation.
- Don't smoke, because it lowers oestrogen levels.
- Curtail your intake of red meat to limit calcium excretion from your bones.
- Limit sodium, because you excrete calcium with sodium.

PAIN MEDICATIONS

Everyone has pain at one time or another and we are all grateful that pain medications are available. However, we all need to take them safely.

- Take with a full glass of water or milk to avoid stomach upsets.
- Know the side-effects of any medication.
- Limit yourself to the weakest dosage and take for the shortest period of time.
- Take your pain medication as soon as the pain begins, not when it is so severe that you may need more to dull the pain.
- Do not take pain medications with sleeping pills. You might not wake up.
- Do not take pain medicine and smoke, because the nicotine in cigarettes alters the metabolism of some medicine.
- Change to aspirin or paracetamol as soon as possible to avoid becoming addicted.
- Try relaxation or ice for your pain before you resort to pain medication.

PARKINSON'S DISEASE

If you notice that someone you love is shuffling or dragging their feet, blinking less frequently than normal and speaking in a very flat monotone, it could be the start of Parkinson's.

Parkinson's results from the degeneration of cells in the part of the brain that produces dopamine, a substance that nerves need to function properly.

- For many, medication will control the symptoms.
- Warm baths and regular massage will aid in reducing muscular rigidity.
- Maintain a safe home environment. (Replace razors with an electric razor, remove throw rugs, light stairways, for example.)
- Simplify everyday tasks. (Replace lace-up shoes with slip-on types, button shirts so that they can be slipped on over the head. Place things used frequently in conveniently located cupboards.)
- Include high-fibre foods in the diet to avoid constipation.
- Increase fluids to aid in soft bowel movements.
- Aid the individual to remain as active as possible, by including regular physical therapy sessions as part of their routine.
- Watch for depression and, if necessary, get professional assistance.

PET-BORNE ILLNESSES

You love your little doggie or pussy-cat. But sometimes they can make you sick.

Pets give love and companionship and occasionally more. There are about 30 varieties of pet-borne illnesses and each year pets pass along infectious disease to thousands. Historically, rabies is the best-known and most-feared pet-borne disease. Most diseases passed from animals to humans are easy to avoid and treatable. Cats and dogs are responsible for the majority of these diseases, but birds, fish and turtles are also common culprits.

- Infections due to bites:
  - ☐ Dogs are responsible for 80 to 90 per cent of bites.
  - ☐ Cat bites cause more infections as they are more likely to carry a virulent organism in their mouths.
  - ☐ Fewer than 5 per cent of dog bites become infected, up to 50 per cent of cat bites do. If you are bitten abroad you will need to obtain an anti-rabies injection immediately. (Check your holiday information.)
  - ☐ Promptly and thoroughly wash any bite with soap and water. More serious bites may require a tetanus shot.
- Dog roundworm and hookworm. The immature form of these parasitic worms can infect humans. You can get roundworm infection by unsuspectingly ingesting the eggs from stool-contaminated soil, hands or objects.
- Make sure your dogs and cats are regularly dewormed.

- Wash your hands after handling a pet or working with soil.
- Cat-scratch disease. This results from a break in your skin, caused either by a cat's claws or teeth. Short of avoiding cats, there is no way to prevent the possibility of cat-scratch disease. However, cats appear to carry the infecting organism for only a few weeks during their lifetime, so the likelihood of being infected by a single pet in your home is minimal.
- Toxoplasmosis. This is a parasitic disease most often acquired from eating undercooked meat, but contact with cat stools may also cause it.
  Caution – Toxoplasmosis is especially dangerous to pregnant women because the organism can cause severe birth defects.
  - ☐ Use rubber gloves when cleaning the litter-tray. Pregnant women should have someone else clean the litter-tray. Wash your hands after handling any cat.
  - ☐ Garden only with gloves because soil may be contaminated with cat stools.
- Intestinal infections:
- Camphylobacter and salmonella, sometimes found in pet stools, can cause acute gastroenteritis. Dogs, cats, birds and turtles cause many cases of gastroenteritis each year.
  - ☐ Cleanliness is your best defence. Wash your hands after handling pets or working with soil.
- Strep infections:
  - ☐ Dogs can carry streptococcus germs in their mouths and show no outward signs of sickness. If recurrent strep throat is a problem in your household, you might consider having your pet examined for the germs.
  - ☐ If the dog is infected, the vet can treat the infection.
- Ringworm. This skin problem is caused by a fungus and is primarily passed to humans by kittens or puppies. It may be unnoticeable because the fungus infects only the animal's fur. It is passed to you when you handle your pet.
  - ☐ Have your vet check any new kitten or puppy for the fungus before you take them into your home.
- Dog and cat mites. A mite is not visible to the eye. It can infect your skin, causing tiny red bumps and intense itching.
  - ☐ Rid your cat or dog of the mites; your vet can recommend the proper insecticide.

None of these conditions are a reason to stop enjoying pets. Taking good care of your pets, having them regularly checked by your vet and following basic rules of hygiene are enough to prevent most pet-borne illnesses.

PHOBIAS

You can't leave your house without your heart pounding and sweat pouring off your forehead. Or, you can't bear the sight of the neighbour's dog, even through the window. Phobias are humorous – but only to other people.

Phobia is a dread of a certain object, place or a situation, and the fear of losing control in the phobic situation. It is considered irrational because the object, place or situation usually is not threatening to others.

- Since the trigger for the physical symptoms are the thoughts that precede it, try to shift the negative thoughts to something positive about the situation.
- Take a chance to expose yourself to the thing you fear a little at a time and give yourself the opportunity to learn that the thing you fear really cannot harm you.
- When you feel a panic attack coming on, do something that you can manage, like taking deep breaths, talking out loud or saying the multiplication tables. Your mind cannot do both things at once and if you concentrate on the manageable task you may be able to gain control.
- Label your fear on a scale of zero to ten. Knowing what increases and decreases your fear may help you to control it.
- When you do function through your phobia, give yourself lavish praise, you deserve it.
- Avoid stimulants such as coffee, tea, cola drinks and chocolate.
- Tensing and relaxing major muscles will aid you in burning up some of the adrenaline you have produced with the phobic attack.

POISON IVY (POISON OAK, POISON SUMAC)

You were only chasing your dog through the undergrowth in a pair of shorts and you didn't feel a thing – until the next day.

Poison ivy creates a skin irritation when the sap of the plant makes contact with uncovered skin. It produces redness, rash, swelling, blistering and persistent, intense itching. The plant is particularly irritating in the spring and early summer when its sap is high.

The first symptom of poison ivy is a burning and itching sensation. This is followed by a rash, swelling and oozing blisters. It is possible to contact the sap by petting an animal whose fur has been brushed by the plant or from the burning of brush by inhaling the smoke from such a fire.

- Wash with soap, lather several times and rinse in running water after each lathering.
- Wash all clothing and equipment that you were wearing at the time of exposure.
- Apply compresses soaked in diluted Burrow's solution or plain hot water. Blisters may be drained but the tops should not be removed. Reinfection can occur by coming in contact with areas of the skin or equipment from which the sap has not been thoroughly removed.
- Apply calamine lotion which has drying properties that will speed healing.
- Use aloe vera gel after lesions are dry to speed tissue repair.
- Take an over-the-counter antihistamine to help control the itching.
- Soak a compress in plain water, cover the rash and then allow a fan to blow on the area – that will also reduce the itching.
- Drink tea of echinacea, goldenseal or myrrh to aid in avoiding infections of the lesions.
- Learn to recognise these plants and avoid them.
- Wear appropriate protective clothing when going through heavy under-growth: long trousers, long sleeves, shoes, socks and gloves.

POSTNASAL DRIP

How charming can you look with your nose like a dripping tap? The sinus and nasal cavities produce moisture 24 hours a day in an effort to keep the air entering your lungs properly humidified. Tiny hairs in your nasal passages keep those places clear but sometimes they slow down because of a cold or because they get dried out. When that happens, secretions form a pool in the back of the throat and you are left with postnasal drip.

- Clear out your nose by blowing it frequently; it will eliminate some of the excess drainage.
- Gargle with salt water, $1/2$ a teaspoonful to a glass of warm water.
- Sniff a similar solution up one nostril at a time.
- Avoid hot and spicy foods.
- Avoid dairy products, as they stimulate the production of mucus.
- Drink fluids. This helps keep the lining of the nose moist and thins secretions so they are easier to move.

- Humidify the air in your house.
- Avoid decongestants; they often create a rebound effect which makes the problem worse in the long run.

POSTPARTUM DEPRESSION

You brought your beautiful baby home, you thought you would be thrilled to be a new mother but now you not only feel overwhelmed, you are wondering if this whole thing is a big mistake on your part. How can any real mother feel this way? You could be suffering from postpartum depression.

Fifteen per cent of new mothers experience this feeling of being overwhelmed and unable to cope. It can last for months and interfere with normal functioning. Following delivery, the new mother's body goes through some tremendous hormonal changes, some hormone levels dropping almost 50 per cent from pregnancy levels.

- Be aware of this change in your body's chemistry and give yourself time to adjust physically. Your thinking may be controlled by your hormones at this time.
- Arrange for some household help so you won't be alone with the new baby and become over-fatigued.
- Nap when the baby naps.
- Plan to leave the baby with a sitter and take some time out away from home with your husband, even if it is only for an hour or two.

POSTURAL HYPOTENSION

Whenever you get up from your easy chair, you feel like the room is spinning and you have to sit down again. You could be suffering from postural hypotension.

- Check your medication. If you take something for high blood pressure, it could be creating the problem.
- Take your time getting up, count to 60 as you get up slowly.
- If you have been sitting or lying down for a long time, move your legs before you try standing to get the blood circulating.
- Try elastic stockings, as they may increase blood flow from the extremities.

POSTURE

Slump along and people will ask you if you're sick. Stand tall, walk with confidence and everyone will know you feel like a million. What kind of a message do you want to send to the world?

Image isn't all of it, however. It is the way to prevent backaches, neck pain and even foot problems. Poor posture wears the discs away – the shock absorbers in your spine – and loosens the ligaments that hold those 33 bony segments together properly protect your spinal cord.

- Begin with basic stretching daily. This corrects any misalignment that has happened during the night.
- If you stand for long periods, raise one foot on an elevated box, and it will release back tension.
- Roll a small towel up and put it into the back of your chair: it will promote good posture while you are seated.
- Sit with your knees level.
- Don't sit with your legs crossed, as it throws your body out of alignment.
- Don't lean on the edge of the table with your elbows, because this encourages slumping.
- Sleep on your side with your knees bent and a firm pillow under your neck.
- Don't sleep on your stomach.
- Exercise to keep your muscles strong which will, in turn, keep your spine properly aligned.
- Look yourself over carefully in the mirror. If you find one shoulder is higher than the other, or some other misalignment is readily visible, practise correcting what you see is wrong.
- Stand with your back against a wall. You should be able to slide your hand between your waist and the wall. You should, however, not be able to get any more than one hand between your waist and the wall. Use the wall occasionally, just to check on your posture.

PREGNANCY

Healthy mothers have healthy babies. If you plan a pregnancy and want to get it off to a good start:

- Have a complete medical check-up before you get pregnant.
- Talk to your doctor about your medications.

- When you decide to have a baby, stop taking birth control pills three months before you plan to get pregnant.
- Maintain a normal weight, lose excess pounds before the pregnancy.
- Exercise.
- Maintain a nutritious diet.
- Avoid caffeine, alcohol, nicotine.
- Don't gain more than two to three pounds a month.
- Relax and avoid stress.
- Take childbirth preparation classes and encourage your husband to take them with you.
- Discuss your views on childrearing with your husband: you may find that you have very differing views which need to be talked about before the baby arrives.

PREMATURE EJACULATION

You were so sexually aroused you couldn't wait and then you found yourself apologising to your partner. You are frustrated and embarrassed and you find yourself dwelling on the thought, "What if it happens again?"

Premature ejaculation occurs when semen is released before penetrating the vagina or immediately afterwards.

- The squeeze technique will aid in delaying ejaculation.
  Firmly pinch the penis directly below the head, using the thumb and first two fingers of one hand for three or four seconds.
- Distract yourself mentally for a few moments, by thinking of other things, if possible.
- Remove yourself from direct bodily contact with your partner, take some deep breaths and begin sexual play all over again.
- Abstain from intercourse for two weeks. Prolong foreplay, stopping just before ejaculation. Continue arousal up to the point of ejaculation with an agreement that there will be no intercourse until the third point of ejaculation.

PREMENSTRUAL SYNDROME

Two weeks before your menstrual period your husband says you turn into a raging maniac. You feel bloated and gain as much as six pounds. You have a backache, headache, more spots and EVERYTHING drives you crazy. Everyone knows to just stay out of your way. Finally, you begin to menstruate and you return to being your old sweet self. Blame it all on PMS.

Premenstrual syndrome is characterised by nervousness, irritability, emotional instability (including outbursts of anger and thoughts of suicide), depression, headaches, generalised oedema and breast tenderness. These symptoms occur during the 7 to 10 days before menstruation and disappear a few hours after the onset of menstrual flow.

This syndrome appears to be related to fluctuations in oestrogen and progesterone and to the fluid-retaining action of oestrogen. During the menstrual cycle changes occur in carbohydrate metabolism (causing low blood sugar) and in the production of various other hormones. Fluid retention affects the blood flow, reducing the oxygen to the uterus, ovaries, and the brain.

- Avoid salt, caffeine, alcohol, dairy products, sugar and all junk food.
- Avoid nicotine as it is a vasoconstrictor.
- If you really crave sweets, substitute your favourite fruit.
- Avoid dairy products. Lactose can block the mineral magnesium which regulates oestrogen.
- Avoid fats, as they help to increase oestrogen levels.
- Avoid salt to decrease fluid retention.
- Do not use diuretics to relieve the bloating. Diuretics remove essential minerals along with the water. Instead, increase your water intake.
- Exercise to increase your blood flow, relax muscles and speed the release of fluids.
- Practise breathing deeply to relieve the feelings of tension.
- Keep to a regular routine to avoid irritability.
- Avoid all caffeine – it has been implicated in breast disease and breast tenderness, as well as contributing to irritability.
- Avoid all cola drinks for the same reason.
- Include high protein foods, broiled chicken and fish in your diet.
- Try a relaxing bath. Soak in your favourite aromatic oil. Take this time to try relaxing and concentrating on letting go of muscle tension.

PROSTATE PROBLEMS

You find that you need to get up in the middle of the night to go to the bathroom. Sometimes, even though you feel like you need to urinate, you can't get a stream started and when you do, there doesn't seem to be much urine. The problem could be your prostate. Unfortunately for men, if you live long enough, you will have an enlarged prostate gland.

The prostate is a gland which surrounds the neck of the bladder and the urethra in the male. It consists of three lobes and is made up partly of glandular matter, the ducts from which empty into the prostatic portion of the urethra, and partly of muscular fibres which encircle the urethra. This is the most frequent site of disorders in the genito-urinary system of the male.

Prostatitis is an acute or chronic inflammation of the gland and is experienced by men of all ages. The usual cause is bacteria from an infection from another area of the body. Prostatitis can partially or totally block the flow of urine out of the bladder, resulting in urinary retention. This causes the bladder to become distended and susceptible to infection as a result of the increased amount of bacteria in the retained urine.

Symptoms of **acute prostatitis** include pain, fever, frequent urination accompanied by a burning sensation, and blood or pus in the urine.

Symptoms of **chronic prostatitis** include frequent and burning pain upon urination, blood in the urine, lower back pain, and impotence. As the condition becomes more advanced, urination becomes more difficult.

Benign hypertrophy. This condition occurs in approximately one third of all men over 50 years of age. It is a result of gradual enlargement of the gland. It can cause disability and even serious illness if untreated.

Symptoms include the need to urinate frequently during the night, as well as pain, burning and difficulty in starting and stopping the urine flow.

Cancer of the prostate. This disease rarely occurs in men under 60. Because the symptoms are usually vague, a large percentage is undetected until the cancer has spread.

- Avoid intercourse while the prostate is inflamed as it may further irritate the gland and delay recovery.
- Do not limit your fluids, as this only increases the problems associated with bladder infections.
- Try asparagine, a health-giving alkaloid found in fresh asparagus. Use a juicer to make a combination of raw asparagus, carrot and cucumber juice. Drink 8 ounces daily.
- A teaspoonful of unrefined sesame oil taken daily for at least one month has been known to aid in reducing an enlarged prostate.
- Eliminate all caffeine and alcohol.
- Try eating some unpressed, unsalted pumpkin seeds daily. They are rich in many of the nutrients essential for prostate health, particularly zinc.

PSORIASIS

People look at those scaly places on your elbows and shrink away from you, afraid that you have some terrible communicable disease. You certainly don't want to go swimming and see people leave the pool the minute you enter.

Your skin cells have gone crazy – you have psoriasis. Normally, skin cells mature and shed after about a month. In psoriasis, this process speeds up, taking only three to four days. The cause is unknown but a family history of the disease is common. Because the lower layer of skin cells divides more rapidly than normal, dead cells accumulate in thicker patches on the skin's outermost layer.

Typically psoriasis flares up for weeks or months; then remits into a period with no symptoms. General health is not affected, except for the psychological stigma of an unsightly skin disease, unless severe arthritis or severe exfoliation of the skin develops.

Mild to moderate psoriasis usually beings as a few red patches of skin covered with silvery scales on elbows, knees, legs, ears, scalp and other parts of your body. In severe psoriasis, patches cover more than half your body and may involve your fingernails, palms and soles.

Onset is usually gradual. The future lesions depend on the extent and severity of the initial involvement and the age of onset. Onset is usually between ages 10 and 40, but no age is exempt. Acute attacks usually clear up, but complete permanent remission is rare. Early lesions are more amenable to treatment than are longstanding ones, but no therapeutic method assures a cure.

- For mild psoriasis, a daily bath can help soak off scales. Because dry skin can worsen psoriasis, don't use hot water or harsh soap.
- Choose an emollient cream that keeps your skin moist. Avoid products containing lanolin which may increase sensitivity.
- Scalp psoriasis often responds to dandruff shampoos. Work up a lather and leave on your head for at least five minutes.
- Phototherapy – even exposing your skin to moderate sunlight may improve some patches, but sunburn may make psoriasis worse. If you have small patches, try a UVB sunlamp.
- Over-the-counter coal tar preparations can be effective on mild psoriasis.
- A cold bath with a cup of apple cider vinegar in it will decrease the itching.
- A bag of ice-cubes held against the skin will also temporarily decrease itching.
- Apply over-the-counter cortisone creams, cover with cling film when you go to bed and you may find that the cells on the surface slow down, but

this is only effective for small areas.
- Lose weight. Although no one knows why, it seems to help.
- Vitamin D3 ointment can improve patches of psoriasis within eight weeks of use.
- Avoid fats, dairy products, red meat, sugar, white flour and citrus fruits.
- Primrose oil or fish oil which are often given for arthritis seem to improve the condition as they interfere with the production of arachidonic acid, a natural inflammatory substance found in red meat and dairy products.
- Linseed oil capsules for unsaturated fatty acid appear to help in some cases.
- Relaxation techniques aimed at reducing stress are beneficial in reducing the incidence of attacks.

RAPE

No one expects to be raped but you can avoid being an easy target if you do some planning. When asked how he chose his victims one rapist replied, "A predator always looks for the weakest creature at the back of the herd." You don't want to be that creature.
- When you move into a new home, change all the existing locks.
- Secure windows and patio doors.
- Pull the curtains after dark so you are not visible from the street.
- Do not open the door to anyone you do not know.
- Do not put your first name on your letter box, your door or in the telephone directory; use your initials.
- Do not enter a lift if there is only one other person in it.
- Avoid dark alleys, do not walk close to doorways.
- Carry your keys in your hand as you walk to your car.
- Keep your car well maintained and don't let the petrol tank get too low.
- Don't give strangers a ride.
- If you feel you are being followed, don't go home. Go to a police station or a public building.
- Don't invite casual friends to your home: meet them in a public place several times first, while you get information about them.

RAYNAUD'S DISEASE

Your fingers are numb and white. Sometimes you feel that your sense of touch is diminished but then your fingers warm up again and the sense of touch returns. You could have Raynaud's disease.

Raynaud's disease is a spasm of the small arteries and arterioles in the fingers and toes (and occasionally other parts such as the nose and tongue), with intermittent paleness of the skin.

The cause in some cases is unknown, but it may be secondary to other disease processes, such as arterial disease, connective tissue disorders, hypothyroid conditions or trauma, such as vibration from using equipment such as chain saws.

In individuals with long-standing disease the skin of the fingers or toes may become smooth, shiny and tight. Small painful areas of gangrene and ulcers may appear on the tips of the fingers or toes.

- Mild cases may be controlled by protecting the body and the extremities from cold.
- Because nicotine is a vasoconstrictor, you must stop smoking.
- Avoid drugs that constrict the blood vessels.
- Avoid caffeine as it constricts blood vessels.
- If the disease is complicated by diabetes, care should be taken to inspect the feet regularly for lesions and the diabetes should be managed.
- Keep the hands and feet warm. Wear comfortable, well-fitting shoes and do not go barefoot. Wear mittens rather than gloves in inclement weather, as they will keep your hands warmer.
- Avoid tight-fitting clothing that can constrict blood flow.
- You can force blood into the fingers. Twirl your arms in a windmill motion for several minutes; it forces the blood by centrifugal force to the fingers.
- Increase your intake of iron-rich foods such as poultry, fish, lentils and leafy green vegetables.
- Manage stress.
- Inspect feet regularly to avoid developing any sores or rubbed spots from shoes. If any develop, pad with moleskin.

RECTAL ITCHING

Well, you certainly don't want to be seen pretending that you are digging your slacks out from between your buttocks in an attempt to scratch and you can't keep excusing yourself to go to the toilet – just to scratch.

Rectal itching is an inelegant, annoying and occasionally embarrassing problem.

It can be caused by haemorrhoids, diet, dry skin, rough cleansing of the anal area or parasites.

If it is more than a temporary problem, you should seek a medical diagnosis.

- Stop scratching – scratching further irritates your skin and leads to persistent inflammation.
- Apply aa ice-pack – this can give immediate, temporary relief.
- Switch toilet tissue – the skin around your anus may be sensitive to coloured, scented toilet tissue or to harsh, less expensive brands.
- Cleanse gently – don't scrub with a flannel: use cotton wool pads moistened with witch-hazel to clean instead of soap.
- Blot dry – or use a hairdryer.
- Watch your diet – if you think foods such as caffeine, nuts or chocolate play a role, avoid them for a few weeks and see if this makes a difference.

RESTLESS LEGS

You are just about to fall asleep when suddenly your legs give a sharp kick, pulling you back from the edge of sleep. Sometimes you feel as if your legs have crawling sensations inside them and you cannot resist the urge to move them.

Millions of people suffer from restless leg syndrome. The cause is unknown but researchers suspect something in the brain's chemistry may be responsible.

- Before you go to bed, take a short walk. This may release endorphins and allow you to relax.
- Move your feet back and forth as soon as the symptoms appear: the movement may interrupt the message to your brain.
- Change your sleeping position.
- Soak your feet in cool, not icy, water before going to bed. It appears to help some people.
- Take one over-the-counter multiple vitamin daily. There appears to be a connection to some vitamin deficiencies in some people.

- Don't eat late at night; a big meal before retiring seems to increase the desire to move the legs.
- Use some techniques to help you relax. Stress seems to worsen the problem.
- Do not become over tired, because fatigue increases the restless leg syndrome.
- Avoid caffeine, because, as a stimulant, it adds to the problem.
- Stop smoking.
- Keep your legs warm outdoors. Constriction of the blood vessels increases the problem for some people.
- Massage your legs just before bedtime.

SALT

The doctor has told you to limit the salt in your diet, but everything tastes so bland without it, you hate to give it up. Salt has been linked to high blood pressure, stroke and oedema.

- Do not add salt while cooking.
- Remove the salt shaker from the table.
- Use low sodium soy, barbecue sauce and other salty condiments.
- Avoid foods prepared with salt brine, such as pickles and olives.
- Limit foods such as smoked fish, kippered herring.
- Try a salt substitute.
- Give food more taste by adding herbs and other condiments such as mustard.

SCARS

If you get a cut, you want it to heal promptly and without scarring. How you treat a cut at first will go a long way in determining how well it will heal.

- Clean any cut properly with an antiseptic.
- Keep the wound slightly moist with an antibiotic ointment while it is healing.
- Don't pick off the scab.
- Apply the oil from a vitamin E capsule over a healing scar and it will probably be less visible when it heals.
- Good wound healing needs good nutrition. Eat properly.
- Clean all scars gently.

- Put sunblock on any scar before sun exposure as they have less pigment than the rest of your skin.
- Allow time to pass. Old scars fade and are less noticeable after time.

SEASONAL AFFECTIVE DISORDER (SAD)

You start to feel depressed in November and don't feel better until the spring comes. Light and temperature play an important role in SAD. Daylight prompts the brain to release chemicals that create feelings of energy.

- Try a full-spectrum fluorescent light, which resembles sunlight.
- Go out as much as possible in the early morning.
- Keep the blinds up in your house or office during the daylight hours.
- Sit near a window, if possible.
- If the weather is very cloudy, turn on all the lights.
- Don't let depression get the better of you. Visit friends, go to the theatre, don't let yourself get isolated.
- Take your holiday in the winter and go to a sunnier clime.

SEBORRHOEA

You have scaly, itchy patches on your face and scalp. One sufferer termed it, 'terminal dandruff'. While it is true you won't die from it, nobody wants to have it.

Seborrhoea is an inflammatory scaling disease of the scalp, face, and occasionally other areas of the body. The disease usually appears only as dry or greasy scaling with variable itching. Yellow-red, scaling elevations of the skin appear along the hairline, behind the ears, inside the ears, on the eyebrows, on the bridge of the nose and the folds alongside it and over the chest.

- Shampoo often. Wash your hair daily if necessary.
- Use a mild, non-medicated shampoo rather than something strong, which can over dry the hair.
- If regular shampoos don't work, then switch to one of the tar-based shampoos.
- Lather twice when you use a dandruff shampoo, then rinse very thoroughly.
- Use a massaging motion on your scalp to help loosen the scales but don't scratch with your fingernails, use fingertips only.
- Use a warm-oil treatment once a week. You will find this treatment

beneficial and it will help to loosen and soften the scales.
- Expose your head to sunshine. Direct ultraviolet light can be beneficial.
- Learn to relax. Anxiety and stress have been implicated in skin conditions such as seborrhoea.
- If the eyelids are involved, a corticosteroid ointment can be applied until improvement occurs.
- A hair rinse made from tincture of chaparall may be beneficial.
- Avoid chocolate, dairy products, fried foods, seafood and nuts as they may all contribute to overproduction of oil glands.
- Keep the skin clean, but do not over cleanse. Avoid harsh cleansers. If you must use make-up, avoid oil-based products.

SECOND-HAND TOBACCO SMOKE

Three thousand non-smokers die from lung cancer a year caused by 'second-hand' tobacco smoke. If you breathe it regularly, you are at risk.

Second-hand smoke leads to coughing, phlegm, chest discomfort, reduced lung function and reddened, itchy and watery eyes. More than 4,000 chemical compounds have been identified in tobacco smoke; at least 43 are known to cause cancer.

Infants are three times more likely to die from Sudden Infant Death Syndrome if their mothers smoke during and after pregnancy.

There is no safe level of exposure to second-hand tobacco smoke.
- If you are exposed, remove yourself.
- If you live with a smoker, pressure them to stop.

SEDATIVES

When you couldn't sleep for a few nights, you took a sleeping pill. After only a couple of weeks, you found you couldn't get to sleep without them. Sleeping pills can be as addictive as alcohol and produce unpleasant withdrawal symptoms if stopped quickly. It is possible to develop a tolerance to sleeping pills in as little time as two weeks.
- Be aware that if you have been taking sleeping pills nightly for more than two weeks, you may be misusing them.
- If you need higher and higher doses to fall asleep, you could be developing a tolerance.
- Avoid increasing the dosage without consulting your doctor.

- Find some alternatives to combat insomnia, such as those listed under *Insomnia*.

SENILITY (SENILE DEMENTIA)

You forgot your car keys and you can't remember whether or not you turned off the stove. You say, "I think I'm getting senile," and everyone laughs but secretly, you are a little worried about how forgetful you are becoming.

Everyone forgets once in a while but the truth is, most people do not become senile.

Senility is a slow disintegration of personality and intellect because of impaired insight and judgement.

The progression of the disease is painful to the beholder, perhaps more than to the patient. Interests become restricted, outlook becomes rigid, conceptual thinking becomes more difficult, and some poverty of thought becomes apparent. Familiar tasks may be performed well, but acquiring new skills is difficult. Initiative is diminished and the patient may be easily distracted. Specific disturbances of speech, motor activity, and recognition of perceptions may become more dysfunctional. Depression is common. Habits can deteriorate, and the individual can become slovenly, dirty and eventually incontinent, culminating with the need for total nursing care in later stages.

Senility may result from a wide variety of pathologic processes. Drugs, depression, deafness, brain tumors, thyroid problems or liver or kidney problems can be some of the causes of senility.

If you are concerned about an older relative, you need to evaluate their lifestyle.

- Often the elderly living alone may neglect nutrition, and evaluation of food intake should be one of the first steps in treatment. Proper nutrition often will solve many of the difficulties in impaired thinking.
- Assistance in the routine of daily living may help.
- A sufficiently nutritious diet is essential, including sufficient protein for normal brain functioning. Older people sometimes evolve into a 'tea and toast' diet.
- Encourage the learning of something new. Curiosity keeps the mind working.
- Play mind-stretching games, such as Trivial Pursuit.
- Encourage reading about subjects of interest.
- Make the person keep lists, that aids in jogging the memory.

- A daily walk will stimulate circulation.
- A diet with sufficient fibre is essential to stimulate bowel function.
- Monitor fluid intake as the elderly do not respond to thirst readily.

SEX AFTER AGE SIXTY

Your man complains, "You aren't interested in sex anymore." What can you do? Or your woman says, "Don't you find me attractive anymore?" What can you do?

Many women experience changes in sexual function in the years before and after menopause. If you were interested in sex and enjoyed it as a younger woman, you probably will feel the same way after menopause. Desire is affected mainly by testosterone, not oestrogen. Women continue to produce sufficient testosterone after menopause to preserve their interest in sex. Oestrogen deficiency may cause a woman's genital region skin to shrink, the opening to the vagina becomes narrower, and the vagina may stay tight and dry. However, sexual arousal begins in the brain, so orgasm is possible throughout your life.

Physical changes in men's response parallel those seen in postmenopausal women. Most men produce well above the minimum amount of testosterone needed to maintain interest in sex. Men with good blood circulation to the penis can attain erections adequate for intercourse until the end of life. Ageing increases the length of time after ejaculation and before restimulation.

For both sexes:

- Use it or lose it: prolonged abstinence from sex can cause impotence. Women who are sexually active have better vaginal lubrication and elasticity of vaginal tissues after menopause.
- Eat healthily – follow a balanced, low-fat diet and exercise regularly.
- Don't smoke – smoking narrows blood vessels, increasing the possibility of impotence.
- Control your weight – moderate weight loss can sometimes reverse impotence. Both men and women will feel more attractive if their weight is within normal limits.
- Limit alcohol – chronic abuse causes psychological and neurological problems.
- Protect against AIDS and other sexually transmitted diseases. The best protection is a long-standing monogamous relationship. If you don't have one, use a condom.

- After age 60 – Intercourse may require planning.

Problem	Solution
Decreased desire	Use mood enhancers. Avoid alcohol. Have counselling.
Vaginal dryness	Use lubricant. Have intercourse regularly. Perform pelvic exercises.
Softer erections	Change position. Accept softer erections as normal.
Erection lost quickly	Emphasise quality, not quantity. Try hugging, stroking, without pressure for intercourse.

SHINGLES (HERPES ZOSTER)

There is sharp burning pain around your body followed by a rash of painful red blisters which later crust over. You are surprised and dismayed, you know you had chickenpox when you were little and you thought that protected you from shingles.

The virus varicella zoster, a member of the herpes family, causes both shingles (herpes zoster) and chickenpox (varicella). Almost every child who grows up in a temperate climate gets chickenpox. Although the disease runs its course over a week or two, the virus is never completely eliminated from the body. Instead, it hibernates in the nerve cells that transmit messages from the skin to the central nervous system.

These viruses may live there quietly for decades. One unlucky person out of five who contracted chickenpox will eventually get shingles, a painful reactivation of the original virus, and a few of those may suffer repeated bouts. No one knows what triggers this reactivation, but it is more likely to occur after the immune system has been worn down by illness, stress, trauma, surgery or simply ageing. The disease can be especially severe for people with AIDS.

Shingles usually starts with pain at the site where it is going to break out, other episodes being with flu-like symptoms: several days of fever, malaise and headache, chills and an upset stomach.

The rash typically develops in strips or bands which follow nerve paths and most often form over the ribs on one side of the body or on a strip on one side of the neck and arm or lower part of the body. Sometimes the rash occurs on the upper half of the face, and the eye may also be affected with a disease called ophthalmic zoster.

Like chickenpox, shingles will usually run its course within a week or two. But unlike chickenpox, shingles may leave painful reminders. As many as half of those over age 60 develop post-herpetic neuralgia. This pain may persist for months or years.

Individuals with shingles are far less contagious than people with chickenpox. This virus is only spread by direct contact with the vesicles. If the vesicles are kept covered they should not be infectious at all. However, for those few individuals who have not had chickenpox, they can catch it from someone with shingles.

- Pain relief comes first. An aspirin substitute may be better for some, aspirin for others.
- Step up your immune system and repair your nerves. Take 200 mg of vitamin C five or six times daily and one vitamin B-complex for nerve repair.
- Leave the blisters alone. Too much rubbing in this area can irritate the skin, making the pain worse.
- Apply a wet dressing made from a damp cloth dipped in ice-water to the affected area.
- Wear loose, cotton clothing. Anything else will make the blistered areas feel hotter.
- Apply calamine lotion or baking soda to the blisters.
- Take a cornflour bath just before bedtime.
- Use over-the-counter capsicin after the blisters are gone. It blocks the production of a chemical that aids in transmitting the pain signal between nerve cells.
- Continue to use ice after the blisters are gone: now put it directly on the area and stroke the skin quickly. This will confuse the nerve signals that send pain.
- Avoid drafts, as they send signals to the nerve endings that will activate pain.
- Allow sunlight on the affected areas for short intervals to speed healing.
- L-lysine, an amino acid available in tablet form, has been shown to aid healing.
- For those in whom the nerve pain lasts long after the illness, therapeutic psychological counselling may help.

SHIN SPLINTS

There is pain and aching in the front of your legs but not in any muscles. You usually feel it after your aerobics class or after standing long hours on an unyielding surface such as concrete.

Most people with shin splints don't do anything about them because the symptoms are rather difficult to describe and they usually aren't incapacitating. It is thought that shin splints may be the beginning of a stress fracture or an irritation of the tendon that attaches muscle to bone.

- Examine the surface you suspect causing the problem. Runners should change to grass, aerobic participants should change to low-impact classes until they feel better.
- Change the surface if you can and then take a look at your shoes. They must support your feet properly and they must fit right. Our feet get larger as we get older and you need to have your feet remeasured regularly.
- Get new shoes frequently, before the soles are gone and while they still have ample cushioning.
- As soon as you have pain, follow the RICE rule.
  R = rest
  I = ice
  C = compression
  E = elevate.
  Prop your legs up, wrap the shin with an elastic bandage, put an ice-pack on for 20 minutes or so, and you'll feel better.
- Stretch your Achilles' tendon and calf muscles – this is particularly good if you are wearing high heel shoes daily.
- Build muscle that surrounds the shin. Try walking around your house barefoot, on your heels only, with the front of your foot pulled up.

SHOE SHOPPING

Your feet are killing you. You've been shopping all day and you have to sit down on a bench, take your shoes off and rub your feet before you can go on. And ... you had better get those shoes back on in a hurry – before your feet swell up and you can't get them back on at all.

- Avoid shoes with pointed toes or high heels. They can lead to such foot problems as ingrown nails, calluses, corns or bunions. High heels force the wearer to lean back to compensate for the forward tilt of the heel, creating spinal problems as well.

- Select laced shoes. They offer more room and adjustable support.
- Wear shoes made of soft leather. Vinyl and plastic encourage perspiration, which can cause problems with the skin of the feet.
- Shop for shoes in the early afternoon. Feet swell as the day goes on. Shoes bought early in the morning may be too tight and shoes bought at the end of the day may be too loose.
- Have your feet measured. Shoe size can change as you age and/or put on weight. Arches tend to relax with age and may require larger, wider shoes.
- If shoes rub anywhere, have them stretched at a cobblers shop.

SIDE STITCHES

You are out for your morning run and suddenly you get a sharp pain, a catch or stitch in your side. Side stitches are caused by a spasm in the diaphragm, the muscle between your chest and your abdomen, which isn't getting the oxygen it needs.

- Stop.
- Massage the area, it will release the cramped muscle.
- Exhale deeply as you massage.
- Get your breathing back to a normal pace, then walk.
- Learn to belly breathe. Become aware of your breathing as you exercise.
- Try to train yourself to have a bowel movement before you begin exercising.
- Do not eat for two hours before strenuous exercise.

SINUSITIS

It drips down the back of your throat. You keep sniffing and snorting but it keeps on dripping. In addition, you have a roaring headache and the pressure seems to just keep building up behind your eyes.

A sinus headache is usually a result of a viral respiratory tract infection. The swollen nasal mucous membrane causes pain in the area over the involved sinus.

- A eucalyptus type ointment can be applied to the forehead and then covered with a cold damp cloth. This will relieve the congestion of the blood vessels in the area and relieve the pain of the headache.
- Use a humidifier; it will keep the mucus moving.

- Bathe your nostrils with a teaspoonful of salt in 1 pint of warm water and a little baking soda. Gently sniff this mixture into one nostril at a time.
- Increase your fluids to keep the mucus thinned out.
- Try an over-the-counter decongestant to constrict the blood vessels.
- Avoid nasal sprays, as they can cause a rebound effect which may make the problem worse.
- Exercise will release adrenalin which will also constrict the blood vessels. Take a short walk, you'll feel better.
- Massage your sinuses. This will stimulate circulation to the area.
- Try eating some fresh horseradish with lemon juice.

SLEEP DISORDERS

(See *Insomnia*)

SMOKING

You know you shouldn't smoke, it is bad for your health and you'd certainly like to quit but you have tried several times and haven't been able to do it.

Mark Twain said, "Quitting smoking is easy. I've done it over a hundred times." You must prepare yourself to quit smoking, both physically and psychologically.

- Begin by altering your self-image. You are a non-smoker, and all that such a person is to you.
- Mark your calendar with the date you intend to be a non-smoker.
- Keep track of each cigarette you smoke.
- Every time you think you will have a cigarette, make yourself wait 10 minutes.
- Collect your stubs in a 'stub bottle'. Keep this bottle in plain sight, as an unpleasant reminder.
- Get rid of all your cigarettes and all the things that you need to smoke, such as matches, lighters and ashtrays.
- Replace the urge to smoke with a deep breath and a piece of hard card.
- Eliminate all familiar smoking cues, such as having a cigarette with coffee. Whilst sipping your coffee, make a list of the things you will do instead, such as taking a walk.
- Keep your hands busy: take up some hobby that requires you to work

with your hands such as knitting.
- Provide oral gratification with sugarless gum or mints.
- Avoid alcohol, sugar and pastries. High sugar items create a biological need that increases your cigarette desire.
- Place a rubber band around your wrist and snap it every time you want a cigarette.

SNORING

You don't believe you snore, nobody does. We all only believe that other people snore – but when your spouse buys ear plugs or moves out of the bedroom – you can be sure that you are a heavy snorer.
- Lose weight. Slimming down often stops snoring.
- Avoid alcohol, it relaxes the throat muscles and contributes to snoring.
- Avoid sleeping medications, they have the same effect as alcohol on snoring.
- Stop smoking, it dries out the throat.
- Sleep on your side rather than your back.
- Use a firm pillow, it will keep your neck in proper alignment.
- Elevate the head of the bed to raise the entire upper torso, not just the head. Put several bricks under the legs at the head of the bed, making sure that the bricks are safely in place.
- Sew a tennis ball into the back of your pyjamas. When you roll over it will help you to remember to stay off your back while you sleep.

SORE THROAT

It hurts to swallow. You keep swallowing to test it, and every time you swallow, it still hurts.

A sore throat can be caused by any kind of irritants that affect the mucous membranes at the back of the throat: allergies, dust, smoke, fumes, extremely hot foods or drinks, infections of the teeth or gums. Chronic coughing and excessive misuse of the voice in yelling or singing, with resultant hoarseness, are frequent causes of sore throats.
- Drink lots of liquids – being well hydrated helps keep mucus thin and easy to clear.
- Gargle with warm salt water – mix a teaspoonful of salt with a glass of warm water to soothe and help clear your throat of mucus.

- Drink honey with lemon juice to coat the throat.
- Suck on a lozenge or boiled sweet, or chew sugarless gum – these stimulate secretions of saliva, which bathes and cleanses the throat.
- Take painkillers. Over-the-counter analgesics (paracetamol, ibuprofen, aspirin) relieve pain for four to six hours .
- Rest your voice. If your sore throat involves an inflamed larynx, talking a lot may lead to more irritations and temporary loss of voice.
- Humidify the air. Adding moisture to the air prevents drying of mucous membranes and the irritation it causes.
- Avoid air pollutants. Stop smoking, avoid smoke-filled rooms and fumes from household cleaners or paint.
- Eat plenty of garlic, a natural antibiotic and antiseptic.
- Change your toothbrush. You may be reinfecting yourself with bacteria that has accumulated on your toothbrush.

SPRAINS

All you did is step off the curb, twist your ankle a little and there you are, with an ankle swollen up to twice its usual size and too painful to walk on.

A sprain is the wrenching of a joint with partial rupture or other injury to its attachments, and without dislocation of the bones. The signs of a sprain are rapid swelling, heat and disablement of the joint. The pain is usually great, and is increased by moving.

- Apply ice-packs to the area as soon as possible. This will aid in reducing the swelling and inflammation. Apply for 15 minutes on, 15 minutes off for the first 24 hours.
- Keep the limb elevated and rest the joint.
- It is best to have an X-ray taken to be sure there is no fracture or broken bones.
- Do not apply weight or pressure.
- After the initial several days, you may use intermittent heat to speed healing.
- An elastic bandage to provide support may be used until the swelling subsides and pain is decreased. Be sure that it is not wrapped too tightly by examining fingers or toes for adequate circulation. This bandage should be removed and reapplied frequently.
- A poultice of turmeric and water can be applied to the area of the sprain under a gauze dressing to reduce bruising and swelling.

- Always warm up adequately before exercising to avoid injury.
- Always cool down after a workout to allow body temperature to return to normal.
- Have proper equipment for your sport or occupation.
- Have proper, well-fitting shoes. Sports such as tennis, football, running and squash should have shoes replaced as soon as the soles appear to be worn down. Examine your equipment frequently for repairs or need for replacement.
- Maintain your home. Worn rugs, stair-rods, ill-lit hallways, inadequately secure handrails in baths – all these can be sources of injuries which could have been avoided.
- Use an over-the-counter painkiller with anti-inflammatory properties to reduce pain.

STAINED TEETH

You have been avoiding smiling because of the coffee or tea stains on your teeth. Or maybe your teeth are yellow from cigarettes and nobody wants to kiss you. Now, that is serious.
- Get a professional cleaning from your dentist.
- Brush regularly, particularly after meals.
- Mix baking soda with hydrogen peroxide and use this to brush your teeth regularly.
- If you can't brush, rinse your mouth with some warm water right after a meal.
- Treat yourself to an electric toothbrush, they have been documented to do a better job than a manual brush.
- Use a soft bristle brush, because it enables you to get around the curved surfaces of your teeth much better than with a hard one.

STRESS

You no longer think ANYTHING is humorous. You snap at the kids, your spouse, and when it reaches the point that you might tell the boss off and lose your job you scream, "I can't take it anymore!"

Stress is the result of long-term anxiety that is not relieved. Almost everyone experiences stress at one time or another in their lives – no one is immune. It can result from a great number of things: job insecurity, high-pressure occupations, relationships, financial problems, loneliness, day-to-day frustrations.

Since everyone experiences stress, it is necessary to learn to deal with it in a constructive manner. The body can handle some stress, whether it is physical or mental. Most people have the ability to do this. If the stress is short-term, then it is possible that each person will be able to cope. It is long-term stress that causes the body to break down.

If symptoms persist for months then the body will respond with physical manifestations of the prolonged stress such as digestive and intestinal disorders. Initial symptoms of stress-related digestive disorders may be an ulcer attack or colitis. Irritability, high blood pressure, headaches, backaches, neck aches, diarrhoea, dizziness and loss of appetite are some of the disorders that can be precipitated by stress. If the stress that produces these symptoms is not relieved then more serious illnesses may result.

Stress seems to express itself when tension or anger or grief graduates from being just one event to being a recurring mood, or even part of the personality. Unrelieved tension actually changes the hormonal biochemistry of your body, encouraging the process of atherosclerosis. Muscular tension squeezes off blood circulation and chronic shallow breathing reduces the amount of oxygen reaching the heart.

- Take a holiday – they are an absolute necessity. Each of us needs to get away from everyday cares and attempt to relax – our mind, our muscles and interrupt the thought processes that keep us worrying and sleepless about things we are unable to change.
- Exercise – physical activity can produce brain chemicals that assist the muscles to relax, the intake of oxygen can aid in transporting blood to the brain to reduce the chemicals that are in operation in stressful lives.
- Rest and get sufficient sleep.
- Deep breathing can be done anytime you are faced with a stressful situation and is a beneficial habit to cultivate.
- Develop a hobby. Find something that can occupy your mind completely separate from the things in your life that are aggravating you.
- Learn to laugh. Loss of a sense of humour is a good indication that your life is too stress-filled.
- If you find you simply cannot handle the stress – you may need professional help.
- Avoid caffeine which aggravates stress.
- Avoid smoking, alcohol and drugs. While they may offer temporary

relief, they actually increase the stress when you have a rebound effect from their use.

- Maintain a good healthy diet to keep your nervous system and immune system in good condition.

STRETCHING

The first thing your cat or dog does upon awakening is a long, slow, delicious s-t-r-e-t-c-h.

A programme of daily stretching can reduce the effects of ageing of muscles and joints. As you age your body gradually loses flexibility. Stretching can help you to maintain flexibility and preserve a full range of motion of all your joints. It will prevent injuries during any activity because it prepares muscles for more vigorous activity.

STROKE

You consider yourself to be quite healthy, you eat well, exercise and go to bed early – but one day your arm felt weak and numb for no apparent reason. Possibly you had a TIA (transient ischaemic attack), a mini-stroke. This could be a warning signal of impending stroke and it is a good reason to go and see your doctor.

A stroke is the result of lack of oxygen to the brain, often caused by atherosclerosis or the rupture of a blood vessel in the brain.

- Control your blood pressure.
- Reduce your cholesterol to below 200.
- Exercise regularly.
- Keep your weight within normal limits.
- Don't smoke.
- Keep your blood sugar levels within normal limits.
- Manage stress.

STYES

It started with just a gritty feeling in the eye and then it blossomed into a bright red, painful sore.

Styes are acute localised infections of one or more glands of the margin of the eyelid.

- Don't poke or squeeze the infected area.

- Hot compresses should be applied for 10 minutes several times a day.
- An antibiotic ophthalmic ointment should be applied for several days to prevent spread of the infection to other locations.
- The hands should be kept clean, rubbing the eyes should be avoided. Take care to avoid transferring the infection to the uninvolved eye.
- Keeping hands and face clean is one of the best ways to avoid such an infection.
- Moistened herbal tea bags: camomile, goldenseal-root applied to the lid as a natural antiseptic are good if you are prone to styes.

SUICIDE

Your friend says, "I just can't take it anymore."

Most people don't mean that, but once in a while, there is one who does.

There is no single cause of suicide. Here are conditions which, alone or in combination, may signal those who are at risk:

Isolation and gender – Men who are separated, widowed or divorced are at highest risk of suicide.

Social status – The higher a person's social status the greater the risk. A sudden change in this status (such as retirement or unemployment) adds to the risk.

Depression – Clinical depression plays a role in about two thirds of suicides in older adults.

Other illness – A serious or chronic medical illness can increase the risk. Older people with **alcohol-related** illnesses are at greater risk.

Misuse of prescription medications is a common suicide method among **older women**.

Many suicides are preventable, if you know the warning signs and then act on them. People who are undecided about living or dying may choose to live if given help.

- Verbal warning – As many as 80 per cent of people who commit suicide give some form of verbal warning of their intentions. Take any talk of suicide seriously.
- Preoccupation with death – Concentrating on death by reading about it or repeatedly turning the conversation to it may signal suicide plans.
- Suicide attempt – Unsuccessful attempts are often followed by successful suicides.
- Unexpected gifts – Giving away valued possessions may be a way of

settling final affairs.

- Changes in behaviour – Increased sadness, loss of appetite, trouble sleeping and inability to concentrate, when severe and prolonged, may signal depression that can lead to suicide.
- Take any warning sign seriously and get help for the person. In urgent situations, call the police.
- Stay with the person contemplating suicide, remove potentially lethal weapons.
- For a less urgent situation, contact the person's doctor or a member of the clergy. Other resources include a mental health centre, a local psychiatrist or psychologist.
- If you are helping someone, be prepared to follow up by making sure they keep appointments for help and support.

SUNBURN

You fell asleep on the beach and now you are paying the price. You can't stand clothing touching your skin and you feel nauseated. You look like a lobster. Soon your nose is going to peel and you are going to look terrible.

Sunburn affecting the lower legs is especially uncomfortable and often slow to resolve. Fever, chills, weakness and sometimes shock may appear if a large portion of the body surface is affected.

Chronic exposure to sunlight has an aging effect on the skin. Wrinkling and yellow discoloration with small yellow nodules are the most troubling consequences.

Precancerous lesions are the consequence of frequent overexposure. Blonds and redheads are particularly susceptible. Squamous and basal cell carcinoma is directly related to the amount of yearly sunlight exposure.

- Don't wait. Take some aspirin or paracetamol right away, it will help relieve the pain, itching and swelling of a mild to moderate sunburn.
- Cold tap-water compresses aid in relieving the symptoms. Apply several times a day for 10 to 15 minutes.
- Mix 1 cupful of skimmed milk with 4 cupfuls of water and then add some ice-cubes. Apply compresses dipped in this mixture; the milk protein is very soothing.
- Oatmeal compresses also soothe the skin.
- Witch-hazel compresses work well also.
- A cool bath with 1 cupful of white vinegar added is good for larger areas.

Pat yourself dry afterwards, do not rub damaged skin.

- Do not bathe with soap if possible. If you do, use mild soap and rinse well.
- Apply moisturiser.
- Over-the-counter hydrocortisone will reduce inflammation.
- Aloe vera gel is very beneficial to healing after the burn begins to resolve.
- Increase your fluids. Sunburn is dehydrating to more than your skin.
- Eat well, as you need skin regenerating nutrients.
- Get some rest. Sprinkle talcum powder on your sheets to minimise friction.
- If blisters develop, leave them alone, they are Nature's bandage.
- After a burn, it takes months for the skin to return to normal. Don't go out the next day and get burned all over.
- Always apply a sunscreen of at least SPF15 about 30 minutes before exposure and be cautious between the hours of 10.00 am and 2.00 pm when the sun is hottest.
- Wear hats, long sleeves for any long exposure such as when doing work in the garden.
- If you must get a tan, do so very gradually, always using a sunscreen to screen out the most damaging of the sun's rays.

SWEATING

You dread someone wanting to shake your hand; your hand is always wet and clammy. Just the thought of having to confront a handshake greeting makes your armpits damp. Levels of perspiration vary widely from one person to another. Sweating and body odour served a purpose centuries ago but we have evolved to a point where our civilisation no longer considers it an asset.

- Use deodorant soap; it will go a long way to make you feel more comfortable about sweating.
- Use an antiperspirant under your armpits as well as on the palms of your hands, two places where excessive perspiration is most visible to others.
- Choose natural fabrics, because they allow perspiration to evaporate.
- If anxious situations cause you to sweat, practise some deep breathing before the situation gets out of hand.

TASTE LOSS

You are complaining how, "things don't taste as good as they used to." If you are adding more salt, eating more sweets, and enjoying your meals less, it could be that your sense of taste is fading.

As you age you lose up to 50 per cent of your taste buds. Perk up your sense of taste by:

- Eating fresh foods instead of canned.
- Using flavour enhancers such as herbs, lemon juice and onions instead of added salt.
- Marinate meat and fish in fruit juice before cooking.
- Include tart foods and beverages in your diet, such as oranges and lemonade.
- Bring foods to room temperature before eating. Chilling reduces flavours.

TEMPOROMANDIBULAR JOINT SYNDROME (TMJ)

When you open your mouth your jaw clicks and pops. Sometimes you have a headache, toothache and finally, it reaches a point where it hurts to open your mouth to brush your teeth. You dentist could diagnose TMJ.

TMJ may be caused by a poor bite, with clenching and grinding of the teeth at night – and stress.

- Sports shops sell a mouth guard for contact sports. Try one to wear while you sleep.
- Limit yourself to soft foods for a brief while and see if that doesn't reduce the symptoms.
- Heat and muscle relaxants may relieve the symptoms.
- Many with TMJ also have back problems, so check your posture. If you lean over a desk, check your body position during the day.
- Try a firm pillow at night, it may help keep your jaw in proper alignment.
- Avoid overextending your jaw when you yawn.
- Do not sleep on your stomach with your head to one side.
- Do not cradle the telephone between your chin and your shoulder.
- Do not carry a heavy shoulder bag.
- Do not work looking up for long periods, such as when painting a ceiling.
- Do wear proper shoes to stabilise your posture correctly.
- Stress management to manage the underlying chronic reaction to on-going

anxiety may be helpful.
- Avoid all high-stress foods such as sugar, chocolate, cola drinks, alcohol and nicotine.
- Exercise to aid in relaxation.
- Get sufficient rest.

TOOTHACHE

It hurts when you drink anything hot or cold and the aching kept you awake last night. You need to see your dentist but you want to do something about the pain until you can get an appointment.
- Rinse with a mouthful of lukewarm water.
- Floss gently to remove any food particles that may be trapped around the tooth.
- Over-the-counter oil of cloves on a cotton ball and held against the tooth is an excellent remedy.
- Avoid biting down on the tooth until you can get to the dentist, because it could be fractured.
- Keep your mouth closed to keep cold air from moving past the tooth.
- Take an over-the-counter painkiller such as aspirin or paracetamol to alleviate the pain temporarily.
- Do not use heat on the jaw until you are certain there is no infection, as heat will only make it worse.

TOXIC SHOCK

You are suddenly struck with a shaking chill, a rapidly rising temperature, a bounding pulse and unstable blood pressure. These are the symptoms of shock.

Toxic shock is potentially fatal. It is caused by the introduction of bacteria into the bloodstream, often through the vagina.
- Use sanitary towels instead of tampons.
- Don't use superabsorbent tampons.
- Don't use tampons with plastic applicators.
- Lubricate a tampon with K-Y Jelly before insertion.
- Change tampons and sanitary towels every four to six hours or more frequently.
- If you use a contraceptive sponge, remove within 24 hours of intercourse.

TRAVEL SICKNESS

The ship rocks gently back and forth. At first you are enjoying the lulling motion but after a while you begin to feel sick and soon you are losing your lunch over the edge and looking very green.

Travel or motion sickness is a functional disorder caused by repetitive motion. It appears that excessive stimulation of the balancing apparatus in the inner ear is the primary cause.

- Children under the age of two and the elderly are usually unaffected by this ailment.
- Think positively. If you believe you are going to be sick you probably will be.
- If you are below decks, get up and breathe some fresh air. Engine odours and other smells can contribute to your ailment.
- Stop smoking and avoid other people's smoke.
- Sail at night if possible. There is less chance of getting sick if you can't see the horizon weaving and rocking.
- Avoid alcohol, as it can set off the symptoms.

If travelling by road, the following may be of help:

- If possible, move to the front of a car or coach and focus your eyes on the horizon.
- Don't read. The motion of any vehicle makes the print on the page move, contributing to your dizziness.
- Chew on ginger sticks, drink ginger tea or sip ginger ale. If taken early enough ginger can prevent vomiting.
- Stay cool, remove excessive clothing and increase ventilation, if possible.

ULCERS

Your favourite food starts a fire in your stomach. You are almost afraid to eat because you know of the pain you are going to experience.

Ulcers are holes or breaks in the inner lining of the oesophagus, stomach or duodenum.

- Try an over-the-counter product containing bismuth which is known to destroy the bacteria thought to be responsible for some ulcers.
- Avoid those foods that you know are going to bring on the pain.
- Avoid milk. While it temporarily buffers the stomach acid, it stimulates more acid secretion.

- Over-the-counter pain medications create more acid. If you take them for something else, such as arthritis, they may be contributing to the problem, so take them with food as a buffer.
- Stop smoking. It has been documented that smoking delays the healing of ulcers.
- Eat little and often, instead of three large meals a day, to keep stomach acids buffered more frequently.
- Eat small meals, avoid skipping meals or going for long periods without food, as food buffers stomach acid.
- Eliminate foods found to cause distress, such as fatty foods, fruit juices and spicy foods.
- Coffee, tea, cocoa, cola drinks and alcohol stimulate acid secretion and should be avoided.
- Fresh cabbage juice has been shown to aid healing.
- Avoid stress, relax. Biofeedback training may be necessary to learn to handle stressful life situations that cannot be avoided.
- Drink plenty of water as this dilutes gastric acid.
- Drink teas of camomile or goldenseal in place of caffeinated drinks, to soothe both nerves and intestinal lining.

VAGINAL DRYNESS

Intercourse has become painful and you find yourself avoiding your sexual partner.

At menopause your oestrogen levels decline, making the vagina dryer.

- Avoid deodorant soaps in the vaginal area, as they are very drying.
- Use a water-soluble lubricant to make intercourse easier.
- Don't douche. The vagina is self-disinfecting and douches can dry out the vagina unnecessarily.
- See your doctor, you may have an infection.